Vladimir
Ilyich Lenin

Vladimir
Ilyich Lenin
Vladimir Mayakovsky

Smokestack Books
1 Lake Terrace, Grewelthorpe, Ripon HG4 3BU
e-mail: info@smokestack-books.co.uk
www.smokestack-books.co.uk

Владимир Ильич Ленин
first published by
Gosizdat, 1925

ISBN 9780995767515

Smokestack Books is represented
by Inpress Ltd

In Memory of
Adolf Aksyonkin

Introduction

Vladimir Ilyich Lenin died at the age of fifty-three on 21 January 1924, after suffering a fatal stroke. Although his state of health had been uncertain for some years, his death came as an enormous blow to the still-fragile Communist Party and sparked widespread grief throughout the Soviet Union. The official government statement, which repeatedly reassured its readers that Lenin's work would continue uninterrupted, nevertheless acknowledged that the news would 'mean a deep shock for every worker and peasant, not only in our Republic, but in all countries'; that 'the working masses of the whole world [would] bewail the loss of their great leader.'[1] Mayakovsky was intensely affected by the news. His friend and lover Lili Brik recalls that

> it was a terrible morning when he died. We wept in the queue in Red Square where we were standing in the freezing cold to see him. [...] I think [Mayakovsky] viewed the body ten times. We were all deeply shaken.[2]

Of the immediate aftermath meanwhile, Mayakovsky's fellow poet and friend Nikolai Aseyev writes:

> Always so lively and reacting directly to everything, Mayakovsky hardly spoke a word in those days. He contracted, as it were, into a single knot of muscles and nerves, so as not to let his genuine, immense sadness erupt and dissipate in external manifestations.[3]

Mayakovsky completed his epic work *Vladimir Ilyich Lenin* in the October of the same year, and it was of huge significance to him. 'Never have I wanted to be understood so much as in this poem', he wrote of it. 'It is probably the most serious piece of work I have ever done.'[4] At 3,000 lines, it is also by far the longest poem he ever published, and it did not come easily. 'I was very afraid of this poem', Mayakovsky writes in his autobiography. 'It would have been easy to reduce it to a simple political summary'.[5]

To some extent the poem *does* act as a political summary – and Mayakovsky undertook a colossal amount of research in order to ensure its accuracy. That this aspect was important to him is made clear from the records of his first performance of it. In response to one of the questions put to him following the reading, Mayakovsky said:

> A comrade is asking here why I have written a course of political education in verse. To this I reply: for the education of those who have not yet been politically educated.[6]

Nevertheless, here too he was careful to emphasise his desire for the work to be recognised as more than just political discourse, explaining that 'poetry is poetry. I remained a poet while writing this poem.' Indeed, having been attacked in the past by some of his peers for writing poetic jingles for State products, Mayakovsky pre-emptively defends the difficult balance of his task early in the poem itself:

> I know,
> your critics'll
> grip their whipsticks,
> your poets
> will go
> hysteric:
> 'Call that poetry?
> Sheer publicistics.
> No feeling,
> no nothing –
> just bare rhetoric!'

Sure,
        'Capitalism' rings
                                not so very elegant;
'Nightingale'
                has a far more delicate sound.
Yet I'll go back to it
                        whenever relevant.
Let stanzas
                like fighting slogans resound!

And *Vladimir Ilyich Lenin* certainly is an ambitious poetical work. It manoeuvres freely from weighty epic intonation to the conversational and the soaringly lyrical, and, despite Mayakovsky's admission that 'Capitalism rings not so very elegant', it is full of the unconventional extended metaphors that are central to so much of his work. The 'sumptuous mansions huddle closer, shivering' in fear at the 'mighty music' of the word 'proletariat', for example, while, as the leader's work gains momentum 'the workers' wrath condenses into clouds, slashed by the lightning of Lenin's pamphlets'. Beyond this, the poem contains some beautiful and highly personal verses which describe Mayakovsky's unbearable pain and disbelief in the aftermath of Lenin's death. 'No sun shone', he writes, 'no ice gleamed pale. [...] Horror! Shut your eyes and blindfold pace the infinity of tight-rope grief'. Mayakovsky's work rarely divides itself neatly into the various constituent parts for which he is known; his agitprop posters and jingles are written with wordplay and wit as much at the forefront as their respective State messages, while even his most explicity indivualistic love poems, such as 'About This', are contextualised by detailed and incisive political critiques. Nevertheless, for Mayakovsky – who was at that time the most famous poet of the Soviet Union – to have produced such a significant piece of writing in a style that maintained his own sense of originality alongside his deep and earnest political commitment, makes *Vladimir Ilyich Lenin* a fascinating and singular work.

For this reason it is interesting that the poem has received such little attention in the west. Only two full translations of it have ever been made into English; the first by Herbert Marshall in 1965, and the second – which has been reproduced for this new edition – by Dorien Rottenberg in 1967. Both have been out of print for over thirty years. In part this is likely due to the western preference for Mayakovsky's love poetry and experimental works over his more manifestly political poems such as this one. Of those published in the Cold War years in particular, certain translators have explicitly acknowledged that their aim was to draw western readers' attention away from Mayakovsky's potentially damaging association with communist orthodoxy, and instead towards his status as an avant-garde formalist writer.[7]

Certainly the particular angle Mayakovsky takes in *Vladimir Ilyich Lenin* is strikingly Marxist in character, even beyond its function as a tribute to the Bolshevik leader. Written in the style of a historical narrative, the poem extends the mortal limits of Lenin's life to incorporate into his biography the history of capitalism and the trajectory of communism, detailing all of the struggles and achievements of the Bolsheviks along the way. However, just as his 'critics' whipsticks' are anticipated in the manifest content of the poem itself, so Mayakovsky is at great pains to weave into his verse an articulation of the way that, in his opinion, Lenin ought – and ought not – to be represented in death. 'I fear these eulogies line upon line', he writes of his contemporaries' verses about the leader, 'like a boy fears falsehood and delusion';

> They'll rig up an aura round any head:
> the very idea –
>   I abhor it,
> that such a halo
>   poetry-bred
> should hide
>   Lenin's real, huge,
>   human forehead.

I'm anxious lest rituals,
                    mausoleums
                                and processions,
the honeyed incense
                    of homage and publicity
should
        obscure
Lenin's essential
                    simplicity.

Indeed, this fear – that Lenin should be held up as an icon in death, a figure of alienation above and beyond the reach of his followers – is not only central to the poem but is what, Mayakovsky suggests, prompted him to begin writing it:

I shudder
            as I would for the apple of my eye
lest Lenin
            be falsified
                        by tinsel beauty.
Write! –
            votes my heart,
commissioned by the mandate of duty.

There are many poets to whom Mayakovsky may be referring with these comments. Within the first five weeks alone following Lenin's death, Wiktor Woroszylski notes that

the National press published poems dedicated to Lenin, written by Bryusov […], Bezimyensky, Vera Inber, Asyeyev, Zharov, Tretyakov, Kamensky, Gerasimov, Dorogochenko, Kirillov, Alexandrovsky, Gorodetsky, Obradovich, Poletayev, Rukavishnikov, and many others.[8]

A good example of the kind of 'poetry-bred halo' to which he objected however can be found in Grigorii Sanikov's poem 'Leniniada'. Full of biblical and apocalyptic imagery, 'Leniniada' describes Red Square being flooded with light as 'from the opened doors, from his dark prison, into the dawn stepped the Leader.' At the dramatic return of this very Christ-like saviour, 'the Kremlin walls fell to the ground' [...] the sun in the sky was eclipsed [... and] thundering rain fell upon the earth.'[9]

However, this opposition to the canonisation of Lenin was not directed solely at Mayakovsky's fellow poets. It was also firmly aimed at the State itself – and this was not the first time Mayakovsky had expressed it. Soon after Lenin's death, the Committee for the Perpetuation of the Memory of V. I. Lenin had sanctioned the production of a proliferation of busts of the leader in various sizes and materials. These busts, which 'falsif[ied]' Lenin with 'tinsel beauty', were heavily advertised by the State Publishing House, Gosizdat, and had already come under criticism from Mayakovsky in the fifth issue of his arts journal *Lef*. Published in the Summer of 1924, this issue contained, in direct contrast to the barrage of sentimental and grandiose verse being produced about Lenin's death at that time by the Proletarian Poets, a series of theoretical articles on Lenin's own use of political language by leading formalists including Boris Eikhenbaum and Viktor Shklovsky. It also featured an editorial article entitled 'Do Not Trade in Lenin', which directly referenced the busts, as well as other commemorative commodities being produced, and implored of the authorities:

We insist:
Don't stereotype Lenin.
Don't print his portrait on placards,
plates, mugs and cigarette cases.
Don't bronze over Lenin,
Don't take from him his living gait and human countenance.
He is amongst the living.
We need him as the living and not the dead.
Therefore

Learn from Lenin but don't canonise him.
Don't create a cult in the name of the man, who all
his life fought against all and every cult.
Don't trade in objects of this cult.
Don't trade in Lenin.[10]

Gosizdat were the distributors of *Lef* and, incensed at this overt attack, brazenly written in one of the journals that they themselves were putting out, they removed the article for publication so that only its title appeared, in the now-inaccurate contents page.

Mayakovsky's assertion that 'we need [Lenin] as the living and not the dead' is made concrete in *Vladimir Ilyich Lenin*. The poem is at pains to describe the leader as 'a boy like any other', a man 'as human as anyone', someone who 'too had illnesses and weaknesses to fight', whose leadership was 'arduous, plain, undramatic'. Mayakovsky accentuates this earthly normality by weaving the lives of the Soviet people into Lenin's biography and promoting the idea that they and Lenin were equals; that their lives were inextricably bound up with his:

I knew a worker –
                    he was illiterate –
hadn't even tasted
                    the alphabet's salt,
yet he
        had listened
                    to a speech by Lenin
and so
        knew all.

If Mayakovsky's opposition to the canonisation of the Soviet leader expresses his stance against that Cult of Personality which began after Lenin's death and became such a central feature of Stalin's dictatorial rule, it also reflects his strict Marxist approach to the practical implementation of communism. Like Marx and Engels, Lenin believed that – as he titled his 1917 article on the subject – 'the State [was] a product of the irreconcilability of class antagonisms', and that

> the liberation of the oppressed class is impossible not only without a violent revolution, but also without the destruction of the apparatus of state power which was created by the ruling class, and which is the embodiment of [...] 'alienation'.[11]

The widespread deification of Lenin following his death ran directly counter to this belief, and *Vladimir Ilyich Lenin* represents Mayakovsky's attempt to provide a more Marxist representation of the leader, alongside a steadfast insistence that it is the commune and not the individul that ought to be the centre of attention following Lenin's death. 'The Party embodies the immortality of our cause', he writes; 'the Party's the compass that keeps us on course, the backbone of the whole working class.' The 'individual', by comparison, '– what can he mean in life?'; 'What's an individual? No earthly good'.

The ideological divergence that is apparent here between Mayakovsky and the organs of the State may be seen as an early marker of those increasingly bitter disputes which arose towards the end of the poet's life. Indeed, in both the case of *Vladimir Ilyich Lenin* and in Mayakovsky's final play *The Bathhouse*, for example, the question of the role of State power in a communist society is central. By 1930, Stalin's totalitarian rule was firmly cemented, and Mayakovsky's scathingly satirical attacks in *The Bathhouse* on the hypocrisy and corruption of the Party, and the self-serving infiltration of State power into every aspect of Soviet life reflect the political futility felt by the poet at that time. In 1924 however, the future of communism still felt alive and malleable to Mayakovsky, and it is this malleability which he is so keen to protect in *Vladimir Ilyich Lenin*.

The poem gained immediate popularity. Marxist critic Kornel Zyelinski describes Mayakovsky's first performance of it, to a crammed audience in the great hall of the Press House on October 18 1924:

Most of the people present were Communists, and there were many people engaged in everyday party work, some of whom had come from the far corners of Russia. [...] Some [...] came here [...] with the desire to criticise sharply what the Moscow personality had written about – what to all those sitting in the hall was dearest and holiest – Lenin. [... But] the closing stanzas were drowned in the warm, sincere applause of the listeners.

As with so much of his work, Mayakovsky came face to face with 'the desire to criticise sharply' from various journalists, critics and Proletarian Poets keen to reject him as a 'true' communist writer,[12] but this professional negativity was drowned out by the overwhelmingly positive reception the poem received from the working people. Describing the success of his reading tour of *Vladimir Ilyich Lenin*, Mayakovsky writes in his autobiography, 'the workers' attitude to it gladdened me and confirmed my conviction that the poem was needed.'[13] Indeed, its cultural significance cannot be underestimated. A recent study, for example, notes that 'many of Mayakovsky's words, torn from the context of [*Vladimir Ilyich Lenin*], gained enormous popularity among the people', and that 'the poet's work greatly contributed to the formation of the political vocabulary of the early Soviet Union.'[14]

In 1930, Mayakovsky was invited to read from the poem at a special event at the Bolshoi theatre to mark the sixth anniversary of Lenin's death. His performance, which was attended by Stalin and his wife amongst other prominent Party members and was broadcast live on the radio, was applauded for a full five minutes and received a standing ovation. In the years following Mayakovsky's death meanwhile, *Vladimir Ilyich Lenin* became by far the poet's most reproduced work, as noted by Chantal Sundaram:

The poema [sic] *V. I. Lenin* appeared in largest numbers: it was printed three times in 1934-35 with a total print run of 70,000 copies. At this time there were still relatively few large poetic works of quality devoted to Lenin, and Mayakovsky's had the advantage of being one of the few such works written shortly after Lenin's death, during the period of widespread mourning.[15]

Of course, given the offical fear around Mayakovsky's 'petty bourgeois individualistic forces'[16], as the Russian *Literary Gazette* put it following the poet's suicide, and of the potential influence of those forces on the Russian people, this editorial choice was no coincidence. In fact, Gosizdat published the rest of Mayakovsky's work irregularly and, for the most part, in tiny expensive editions, effectively making his more experimental and politically critical poems impossible to get hold of by Soviet readers, and inaccurately establishing him as the officially sanctioned poet of Stalin's Russia.

From this perspective it is little wonder then that western Cold War translators were so keen to redress the balance by prioritising Mayakovsky's lyrical works. Interestingly however, despite a new willingness among Twenty-First Century translators and critics to acknowledge Mayakovsky's status as a Marxist poet[17], *Vladimir Ilyich Lenin* remains relatively unknown in the west. In contemporary Russia, the poet's legacy has benefitted from a huge post-Soviet resurgence of interest in his avant-garde, lyrical poems – it is now 'A Cloud in Trousers', for example, which is taught in schools, and not 'My Soviet Passport' – but *Vladimir Ilyich Lenin* is still firmly recognised as one of the poet's most significant works. Why then, is no one prepared to take it on in the English language?

Comparing Marshall and Rottenberg's translations offers some insight into this question. At times, in both cases, the sheer length of the poem alongside its ambitious scope has made maintaining momentum difficult. Meanwhile, their attempts to mirror the regular rhyme scheme which in Mayakovsky's deft and flexible language works well have, in our more unwieldy tongue, forced them into some unnatural-sounding contortions. For example, the lines:

Plyunem v litso
                       toi beloi slyakoti,
syusyukayushchei
                       o zverstvax Cheka!
Smotrite,
          kak zdes',
                       svyazavshi zá lokti,
rabochih násmert'
                       sekli po shchekam.

are translated by Marshall as:

We spit in the face
                       of that white scum,
lisping
       of the Cheka's brutality!
See,
     how here,
               with arms bound behind them,
workers are beaten to death
                       cold-bloodedly.[18]

These lines are translated more naturally by Rottenberg:

Spit in the faces
                       of white dross who tell us
about the Cheka's
                       blood-dousings!
They ought to have seen
                       how, tied by the elbows,
workers
        were flogged to death
                       by thousands.

However, Rottenberg also strains to organise his language around the unforgiving rhyme scheme throughout the poem. For example, we have the rather awkward-sounding:

Lenin and the Party
                    are brother-twins.
Who'll say which means more
                    to History – their mother?
Lenin
      and the Party
                    are the closest kin;
name one
         and you can't but imply
                    the other

Meanwhile, in the excerpt below, the poetic syntax feels exceptionally stilted and forced:

To all,
        every
              and each,
slaves of the rich
                   one another
                              hacking and carving;
to you we appeal
                this hour
Let the Soviets
               take over government power!

Nevertheless, of the two that exist, it is Rottenberg's version which is the most fluid and lively. Although it is certainly not without its faults, it represents a remarkable contribution to Mayakovsky's translated works, and the value of having it available in print for English-speaking readers far outweighs the occasional clunkiness of expression in its delivery. As both an intrinsic element of Mayakovsky's immense and impressive canon of work, and as a nuanced and powerful artefact of early Soviet cultural history, *Vladimir Ilyich Lenin* is an enormously important work, and it is with great delight that I am able to restore it to print in this new edition.

Rosy Carrick, 2017

Notes

1   This statement was printed in a special issue of the newspapers *Pravda* and *Izvestiya* on Jan 22 1924. In Wictor Woroszylski, *The Life of Mayakovsky*, trans. Boleslaw Taborski (New York: The Orion Press, 1971), pp. 341-342.

2   In Bengt Jangfeldt, *Mayakovsky: A Biography*, trans. Harry D. Watson (Chicago and London: The University of Chicago Press, 2015), pp. 284-285.

3   Recorded in Woroszylski, *The Life*, p. 342.

4   Cited in the introduction to Rosy Carrick, ed., *Volodya* (London: Enitharmon, 2015), p. 14.

5   From 'Я сам' ('I, Myself'), Vladimir Mayakovsky, *Полное собрание сочинений Том 1*, ed. V.A. Katanyan (Moscow: Gos. Izd. Khud. Lit., 1955-61), p. 27. My translation.

6   Kornel Zyelinsky, in Woroszylski, *The Life*, p. 347.

7   See 'Introduction', *Volodya*, pp. 14-15.

8   Woroszylski, *The Life*, pp. 342-343.

9   Quoted by Mark D. Steinberg in *Proletarian Imagination: Self, Modernity, and the Sacred in Russia, 1910-1925* (Ithaca and London: Cornell University Press, 2002), pp. 275-276. 'Leniniada' was not published in its entirety until 1925, but fragments appeared soon after Lenin's death.

10   Quoted in Peter Jukes, *A Shout in the Street: An Excursion Into the Modern City* (Berkley and Los Angeles, University of California Press, 1990),p. 156.

11   Vladimir Ilyich Lenin, *The State and Revolution* Chapter 1: 'The State: A Product of the Irreconcilability of Class Antagonisms', Collected Works Vol. 25.

12   There were many instances of such criticism, but for an interesting example, see Vissarion Sayanov's account of Mayakovsky's treatment by Proletarian Poet Demyan Bedney and journalist Lev Sosnovsky at the first conference of proletarian writers in 1925. Recorded in Woroszylski, *The Life*, pp. 353-356.

13   'I Myself', trans. Herbert Marshall in *Mayakovsky* (New York: Hill and Wang, 1965), p. 91.

14   Kharlanovich Olesya Petrovna and Dolzhenko Natalia Grigorievna, 'Linguistic Features of the Political Discourse of the Early Soviet Union in the example of Vladimir Mayakovsky's Work', *The Youth Scientific Forum: Humanities* (5:44): 2017. The language in question includes both neologisms such as Mayakovsky's phrase 'голодный и голоштанный' ('hungry and hollow'), and his slogan-like statements, such as 'When we say Lenin – what we mean is the Party, when we say the Party – what we mean is Lenin').

15 Chantal Sundaram, *Manufacturing culture, the Soviet state and the Mayakovsky legend, 1930-1993* (Ottawa: National Library of Canada, 2001), pp. 114-115.

16 Quoted in Michael Holquist, 'The Mayakovsky Problem', in *Yale French Studies* 39 (1967): p. 132.

17 Harry Gilonis's collection *For British Workers* (Barque 2015) emphasises Mayakovsky's Marxist status by devoting itself entirely to Mayakovsky's political poetry for example, while *Volodya* promotes it by including never before-translated political works alongside his more well-known lyrical poems.

18 Marshall, *Mayakovsky*, pp. 286-287.

Российской
коммунистической партии
посвящаю

To the Russian
    Communist Party
        I dedicate this poem

Время –
        начинаю
             про Ленина рассказ.
Но не потому,
          что горя
                нету более,
время
     потому,
         что резкая тоска
стала ясною
          осознанною болью.
Время,
     снова
          ленинские лозунги развихрь.
Нам ли
     растекаться
           слезной лужею, –
Ленин
     и теперь
          живее всех живых.
Наше знанье –
       сила
          и оружие.
Люди – лодки.
        Хотя и на суше.
Проживешь
       свое
          пока,
много всяких
          грязных ракушек
налипает
       нам
         на бока.

The time has come.
                    I begin
                            the story of Lenin.
Not because
            the grief
                        is on the wane,
but because
            the shock
                        of the first moment
has become a clear-cut,
                            weighed and fathomed pain.
Time,
     speed on,
                spread Lenin's slogans in your whirl!
Not for us
            to drown in tears,
                                whatever happens.
There's no one
                more alive
                            than Lenin in the world,
our strength,
            our wisdom,
                            surest of our weapon.
People are boats,
                    albeit on land.
While life
            is being
                    roughed
all species of trash
                        from the rocks and sand
 stick
     to the sides
                    of our craft.

А потом,
            пробивши
                        бурю разозленную,
сядешь,
            чтобы солнца близ,
и счищаешь
            водорослей
                        бороду зеленую
и медуз малиновую слизь.
Я
   себя
            под Лениным чищу,
чтобы плыть
            в революцию дальше.
Я боюсь
            этих строчек тыщи,
как мальчишкой
                        боишься фальши.
Рассияют головою венчик,
я тревожусь,
                        не закрыли чтоб
настоящий,
            мудрый,
                        человечий
ленинский
            огромный лоб.
Я боюсь,
            чтоб шествия
                        и мавзолеи,
поклонений
            установленный статут
не залили б
            приторным елеем
ленинскую
            простоту.

But then,
        having broken
                        through the storm's mad froth,
one sits
        in the sun for a time
and cleans off
            the tousled seaweed growth
                                and oozy
jellyfish slime.
I
  go to Lenin
            to clean off mine
to sail on
        with the revolution.
I fear
        these eulogies line upon line
like a boy
            fears falsehood and delusion.
They'll rig up an aura round any head:
the very idea –
                I abhor it,
that such a halo
                poetry-bred
should hide
            Lenin's real, huge,
                            human forehead.
I'm anxious lest rituals,
                    mausoleums
                                and processions,
the honeyed incense
                of homage and publicity
should
        obscure
Lenin's essential
                simplicity.

За него дрожу,
                как за зеницу глаза,
чтоб конфетной
                не был
                        красотой оболган.
Голосует сердце –
                я писать обязан
по мандату долга.

*   *   *

Вся Москва.
        Промерзшая земля
                        дрожит от гуда.
Над кострами
        обмороженные с ночи.
Что он сделал?
                Кто он
                        и откуда?
Почему
        ему
                такая почесть?
Слово за словом
                из памяти таская.
не скажу
        ни одному –
                        на место сядь.
Как бедна
        у мира
                слова мастерская!
Подходящее
        откуда взять?

I shudder
        as I would for the apple of my eye
lest Lenin
       be falsified
             by tinsel beauty.
Write! –
      votes my heart,
commissioned by the mandate of duty.

* * *

All Moscow's
       frozen through,
             yet the earth quakes with emotion.
Frostbite
     drives its victims to the fires.
Who is he?
       Where from?
            Why this commotion?
Why
   such honours
          when a single man expires?
Dragging word by word
           from memory's coffers
won't suit
     either me
         or you who read.
Yet what a meagre
        choice
          the dictionary offers!
Where to get
      the very words we need?

29

У нас
        семь дней,
у нас
        часов – двенадцать.
Не прожить
            себя длинней.
Смерть
        не умеет извиняться.
Если ж
        с часами плохо,
мала
        календарная мера,
мы говорим –
                «эпоха»,
мы говорим –
                «эра».
Мы
    спим
            ночь.
Днем
        совершаем поступки.
Любим
        свою толочь
воду
        в своей ступке.
А если
        за всех смог
направлять
                потоки явлений,
мы говорим –
                «пророк»,
мы говорим –
                «гений».

We've
          seven days to spend,
twelve hours
                    for diverse uses.
Life must begin –
                         and end.
Death
          won't accept excuses.
But if
       it's no more
                      a matter of hours,
if the calendar measure
                              falls short,
'Epoch'
            is a usual comment of ours,
'Era' or something of the sort.
We
      sleep
            at night,
busy
       around by day,
each grinds his water
                          in his own pet mortar
and so
        fritters life away.
But if,
        single-handed,
                           somebody can
turn the tide
              to everyone's profit
we utter something like
                           'Superman',
'Genius'
          or 'Prophet'.

У нас
          претензий нет, –
не зовут –
               мы и не лезем;
нравимся
          своей жене,
и то
          довольны донельзя.
Если ж,
          телом и духом слит,
прет
          на нас непохожий,
шпилим –
               «царственный вид»,
удивляемся –
               «дар божий».
Скажут так, –
               и вышло
                         ни умно, ни глупо.
Повисят слова
               и уплывут, как ды́мы.
Ничего
          не выколупишь
                         из таких скорлупок.
Ни рукам
          ни голове не ощутимы.
Как же
          Ленина
               таким аршином мерить!
Ведь глазами
               видел
                    каждый всяк –
«эра» эта
          проходила в двери,
даже
     головой
          не задевая о косяк.

We
    don't ask much of life,
won't budge an inch
                    unless required.
To please
        the wife
is the utmost
            to which we aspire.
But if,
    monolithic in body and soul,
someone
        unlike us
                    emerges,
we discover
            a god-like aureole
or appendages
                equally gorgeous.
Tags and tassels
                laid out on shelves,
neither silly
        nor smart –
                    no weightier than smoke.
Go
    scrape meaning
                    out of such shells –
empty as eggs
            without white or yolk.
How, then, apply
                such yardsticks to Lenin
when anyone could see
                    with his very own eyes:
that 'era'
        cleared doorways
                        without even bending,
wore jackets
        no bigger
                than average size.

Неужели
       про Ленина тоже:
«вождь
       милостью божьей»?
Если б
     был он
            царствен и божествен,
я б
   от ярости
         себя не поберег
я бы
    стал бы
       в перекоре шествий,
поклонениям
        и толпам поперек.
Я б
   нашел
      слова
         проклятья громоустого,
и пока
    растоптан
        я
         и выкрик мой,
я бросал бы
      в небо
         богохульства,
по Кремлю бы
      бомбами
        метал:
          д о л о й!
Но тверды
     шаги Дзержинского
         у гроба.

Should Lenin, too,
                    be hailed by the nation
as 'Leader
          by Divine Designation'?
Had he
      been kingly
                  or godly indeed
I'd
    never spare myself,
                      on protest bent;
I'd
    raise a clamour
                  in hall and street
against the crowds, speeches,
                              processions and laments.
I'd
    find
        the words
                  for a thundering condemnation,
and while
          I'd be trampled on,
                              I
                                and my cries,
I'd bomb
        the Kremlin
                    with demands for resignation,
hurling
        blasphemy
                  into the skies.
But calm
        by the coffin
                      Dzerzhinsky appears.

Нынче бы
                могла
                        с постов сойти Чека.
Сквозь мильоны глаз,
                        и у меня
                                сквозь оба,
лишь сосульки слез,
                        примерзшие
                                к щекам.
Богу
        почести казенные
                        не новость.
Нет!
        Сегодня
                настоящей болью
                        сердце холодей.
Мы
        хороним
                самого земного
изо всех
        прошедших
                по земле людей.
Он земной,
        но не из тех,
                кто глазом
упирается
        в свое корыто.
Землю
        всю
        охватывая разом.
видел
        то,
        что временем закрыто.

Today
    he could easily
                 dismiss the guard.
In millions of eyes
            shines nothing
                      but tears,
not running
       down cheeks,
              but frozen hard.
Your divinity's decease
             won't rouse
                 a mote of feeling.
No!
   Today
      real pain
           chills every heart.
We're burying
      the earthliest
           of beings
that ever came
      to play
         an earthly part.
Earthly, yes:
      but not the earth-bound kind
                who'll never peer
beyond the precincts
      of their sty.
He took in
    all the planet
        at a time,
saw things
    out of reach
        for the common eye.

Он, как вы
       и я,
           совсем такой же,
только,
      может быть,
           у самых глаз
мысли
     больше нашего
             морщинят кожей,
да насмешливей
        и тверже губы,
             чем у нас.
Не сатрапья твердость,
             триумфаторской коляской
мнущая
    тебя,
        подергивая вожжи.
Он
  к товарищу
       милел
          людскою лаской.
Он
   к врагу
      вставал
         железа тверже.
Знал он
     слабости,
         знакомые у нас,
как и мы,
      перемогал болезни.
Скажем,
     мне бильярд –
            отращиваю глаз,
шахматы ему –
      они вождям
          полезней.

Though like you
                and I
                        in every detail,
his forehead rose
                a taller,
                        steeper tower;
the thought-dug wrinkles
                        round the eyes
                                went deeper,
the lips looked firmer,
                more ironical
                        than ours.
Not the satrap's firmness
                        that'll grind us,
tightening
        the reins,
                beneath a triumph-chariot's wheel.
With friends
        he'd be
                the very soul
                        of kindness,
with enemies
        he'd be
                as hard
                        as any steel.
He, too,
        had illnesses
                and weaknesses to fight
and hobbies
        just the same as we have, reader.
For me
        it's billiards, say,
                        to whet the sight;
for him it's chess –
                more useful
                        for a leader.

И от шахмат
            перейдя
                  к врагу натурой,
в люди
       выведя
               вчерашних пешек строй,
становил
         рабочей – человечьей диктатурой
над тюремной
               капиталовой турой.
И ему
     и нам
           одно и то же дорого.
Отчего ж,
        стоящий
               от него поодаль,
я бы
     жизнь свою,
             глупея от восторга,
за одно б
       его дыханье
             óтдал?!
Да не я один!
         Да что я
             лучше, что ли?!
Даже не позвать,
          раскрыть бы только рот –
кто из вас
       из сёл,
          из кожи вон,
             из штолен
не шагнет вперед?!
В качке –
       будто бы хватил
               вина и горя лишку –
инстинктивно
        хоронюсь
            трамвайной сети.

And turning
              face about from chess
                              to living foes,
yesterday's dumb pawns
                      he led
                              to a war of classes
until a human, working-class dictatorship
                                      arose
to checkmate Capital
                  and crush its prison-castle.
We
    and he
          had the same ideals to cherish.
Then why is it,
              no kin of his,
                          I'd welcome death,
crazy with delight,
                  I would
                          gladly perish
so that
      he might draw
                  a single breath?
And not I alone.
              Who says
                      I'm better than the rest?
Not a single soul of us,
                      I reckon,
in all the mines
              and mills
                      from East
                              to West
would hesitate to do the same at the slightest beckon.
Instinctively,
            I shrink from tram-rails
                                  to quiet corners,
giddy
    as a drunk
              who sees the lees.

Кто
        сейчас
              оплакал бы
                    мою смертишку
в трауре
        вот этой
              безграничной смерти!
Со знаменами идут,
              и так.
                    Похоже –
стала
      вновь
            Россия кочевой.
И Колонный зал
              дрожит,
                    насквозь прохожен.
Почему?
      Зачем
            и отчего?
Телеграф
        охрип
              от траурного гуда.
Слезы снега
        с флажьих
              покрасневших век.
Что он сделал,
        кто он
              и откуда –
этот
      самый человечный человек?

                    *   *   *

Who
    would mind
           my puny
               death
among these mourners
            lamenting
                 the enormousness of his decease?
With banners
       and without,
            they come,
as if all Russia
       had again
            turned nomad for a while.
The Hall of Columns
            trembles
               with their motion.
What can be the reason?
            Wherefore?
               Why?
Snow-tears
       from the flags' red eyelids
                 run.
The telegraph's
       gone hoarse
            with humming mournful rumours.
Who is he?
       Where from?
            What has he done,
this man,
       the most humane of all us humans?

*   *   *

Коротка
        и до последних мгновений
нам
    известна
        жизнь Ульянова.
Но долгую жизнь
           товарища Ленина
надо писать
        и описывать заново.
Далеко давным,
        годов за двести,
первые
    про Ленина
        восходят вести.
Слышите –
    железный
        и луженый,
прорезая
       древние века, –
голос
    прадеда
        Бромлея и Гужона –
первого паровика?
Капитал
    его величество,
           некоронованный,
               невенчанный,
объявляет
    покоренной
        силу деревенщины.

Ulyanov's short life
                    is known
to men in
        every country
                        among every race.
But the longer biography
                        of Comrade Lenin
has still to be written,
                    rewritten and retraced.
Far, far back,
            two hundred years or so,
the earliest
        beginnings
                    of Lenin go.
Hear those brazen,
                peremptory
                            tones
With their century-piercing
                        motif?
It's the grandfather
                of Bromley's and Goujon's,
the first
        steam locomotive.
Capital,
        His Majesty,
                    uncrowned,
                                as yet unknown,
declares
        the gentry's power
                        overthrown.

Город грабил,
              грёб,
                     грабастал,
глыбил
        пуза касс,
а у станков
              худой и горбастый
встал
        рабочий класс.
И уже
        грозил,
              взвивая трубы зá небо:
– Нами
        к золоту
              пути мостúте.
Мы родим,
        пошлем,
                     придет когда-нибудь
человек,
        борец,
              каратель,
                     мститель! –
И уже
        смешались
              облака и дúмы,
будто
        рядовые
              одного полка.
Небеса
        становятся двойными,
дымы
        забивают облака.
Товары
        растут,
              меж нищими высясь.

The city pillaged,
                plundered,
                            pumped gold
into the bellies
                of banks,
while at the workbenches,
                            lean and humped,
the working class
                closed ranks.
And already
            threatened,
                            rearing smokestacks to the sky,
'Pave your way with us
                    to fortunes,
                                grip us tighter!
But remember:
            he is coming,
                        he is nigh,
the Man,
        the Champion,
                    the Avenger,
                                the Fighter!'
And already
            smoke and clouds
                            get mixed together
as when mutineers
                turn orderly detachments
                                    into crowds,
until
    the tokens
of a storm
        begin to gather –
the sky
        brews trouble –
                    ugly smoke blacks out the clouds.

Директор,
        лысый черт,
пощелкал счетами,
                буркнул:
                        «кризис!»
и вывесил слово
                «расчет».
Крапило
        сласти
                мушиное се́ево,
хлеба̀
        зерном
                в элеваторах портятся,
а под витринами
                всех Елисеевых,
живот подведя,
                плелась безработица.
И бурчало
        у трущоб в утробе,
покрывая
        детвориный плачик:
– Под работу,
        под винтовку ль,
                на́ –
                        ладони обе!
Приходи,
        заступник
                и расплатчик!

*   *   *

Amid beggars
              a mountain of goods arises.
The manager, bald beast,
                    flips his abacus,
                              blurts out 'crisis!'
and pins up a list:
                    'DISMISSED:..'
Fly-blown
           pastries in dustbins
                         found graves,
grain –
       in granaries
                 with mildew cloyed,
while past the windows
                   of Yeliseyev's,
belly caved in,
              shuffled the unemployed.
And the call
           came rumbling from shack and slum,
covering
       the whimper of kiddies:
'Come,
       protector!
                 Redresser,
                           come!
And we'll go
           to battle
                   or wherever you bid us!'

*   *   *

Эй,
   верблюд,
         открыватель колоний! -
Эй,
   колонны стальных кораблей!
Марш
     в пустыни
         огня раскаленней!
Пеньте пену
      бумаги белей!
Начинают
      черным латáться
оазисы
      пальмовых нег.
Вон
   среди
       золотистых плантаций
засеченный
       вымычал негр:
– У-у-у-у-у,
      у-у-у!
           Нил мой, Нил!
Приплещи
     и выплещи
         черные дни!
Чтоб чернее были,
       чем я во сне,
и пожар чтоб
        крови вот этой красней.
Чтоб во всем этом кофе,
           вразь, вскипелом,
вариться пузатым –
        черным и белым.
Каждый
     добытый
        слоновий клык –
тык его в мясо,
       в сердце тык.

Hey,
    camel,
            discoverer of colonies!
Ahoy,
      caravans of steel-hulled ships!
March
        through the desert,
                            fire-like scalding,
cleave through the billows
                            on east-bound trip!
Shadows
         of ominous ugly black
start patching the sky
                      over sun-kissed oases.
Hear the Negro
            with whip-lashed back
                                    muttering
among the bananas
                and maizes:
'Oo-oo,
        oo-oo,
              Nile, my Nile!
Splash up a day
              like a crocodile,
                                let it be blacker
than I at night.
              With fire
like my blood,
                as red and as bright,
for the fattest bellies
                    both white and black
to fry and sizzle,
                to split and crack!
Each
    and every
              ivory tusk
hack and poke them
                from dawn to dusk.

Хоть для правнуков,

                не зря чтоб

                        кровью литься,

выплыви,

           заступник солнцелицый.

Я кончаюсь, –

           бог смертей

                        пришел и поманил.

Помни

        это заклинанье,

                Нил,

                   мой Нил! –

В снегах России,

           в бреду Патагонии

расставило

        время

               станки потогонные.

У Иванова уже

          у Вознесенска

                  каменные туши

будоражат

        выкрики частушек:

«Эх, завод ты мой, завод,

желтоглазина.

Время нового зовет

Стеньку Разина».

                      *   *   *

Don't let me bleed in vain –
                              if only for descendants
                                             come,
O Sun-Faced,
           deal out justice and defend us!
I'm through;
           the God of deaths won't wait –
                              I've lived my while.
Mind
     my incantation,
                    Nile,
                      my Nile!'
From snow-bound Russia
                     to sun-scorched Patagonia
mechanical sweat-mills
                  went grinding
                             and groaning.
In Ivanovo-
          Voznesensk,
                    the loom-twirling city,
brickwork mammoths
                  shook with the ditty:
'Cotton-mill, my cotton-mill,
Gins and looms a-buzzin',
It's high time he came along,
Another Stenka Razin!'

                    *   *   *

Внуки
      спросят:
            – Что такое капиталист? –
Как дети
      теперь:
            – Что это
                     г-о-р-о-д-о-в-о-й?.. –
Для внуков
      пишу
          в один лист
капитализма
        портрет родовой.
Капитализм
       в молодые года
был ничего,
        деловой парнишка:
первый работал –
           не боялся тогда,
что у него
      от работ
           засалится манишка.
Трико феодальное
        ему теснò!
Лез
   не хуже,
        чем нынче лезут.
Капитализм
       революциями
           своей весной
расцвел
     и даже
         подпевал «Марсельезу».

Grandsons
        will ask,
                'What does Capitalism mean?'
just as kiddies
            today,
                'What's a
                        gendarme, Dad?'
So here's
        capitalism
                as then he was seen,
portrayed
        for grandsons full-size in my pad.
Capitalism
        in his early years
wasn't so bad –
                a business-like fellow.
Worked like the blazes –
                        none of those fears
that his snowy cravat
                would soil
                        and turn yellow.
Feudal tights
        felt too tight for the youngster;
forged on
        no worse
                than we do these days;
raised revolutions
                and
                    with gusto
joined
    his voice
            in the *Marseillaise*.

Машину
       он
            задумал и выдумал.
Люди,
      и те – ей!
Он
   по вселенной
                  видимо-невидимо
рабочих расплодил
              детей.
Он враз
      и царства
              и графства сжевал
с коронами их
         и с орлами.
Встучнел,
      как библейская корова
                    или вол,
облизывается.
         Язык – парламент.
С годами
      ослабла
          мускулов сталь,
он раздобрел
       и распух,
такой же
     с течением времени
                 стал,
как и его гроссбух.
Дворец возвел –
         не увидишь такого!
Художник
     – не один! –
         по стенам поерзал.

Machines
          he
              spawned from his own smart head
and put new slaves
                    to their service:
million-strong broods
                    of workers
                                    spread
all over
        the world's surface.
Whole kingdoms
                and counties
                                  he swallowed at a time
with their crowns and eagles
                                and suchlike ornaments,
fattening up
            like the biblical kine,
                                    licking
his chops,
            his tongue –parliament.
But weaker
            with years
                        his limb-steel became,
he swelled up
              with leisure and pleasure,
gaining in bulk
                and weight
                                the same
as his own beloved ledger.
He built himself palaces
                          ne'er seen before.
Artists –
          hordes of 'em –
                          went through their chores.

Пол ампиристый,
                потолок рококóвый,
стенки –
        Людовика XIV,
                    Каторза.
Вокруг,
    с лицом,
            что равно годится
быть и лицом
            и ягодицей,
задолицая
        полиция.
И краске
        и песне
                душа глуха,
как корове
        цветы
            среди луга.
Этика, эстетика
                и прочая чепуха –
просто –
        его
            женская прислуга.
Его
    и рай
        и преисподняя –
распродает
            старухам
дырки
        от гвоздей
                    креста господня
и перо
        хвоста
            святого духа.

Floors – à l'Empire,
                    ceilings – Rococo,
walls –
      Louis XIV,
                  Quatorze.
Around him
            with faces
                      equally fit
to be faces
            or the places on which they sit,
keeping the peace,
                  stood buttock-faced police.
His soul
      to song
            and to colour insensate –
like a cow
        in a meadow
                    abloom with flowers –
ethics and aesthetics
                    his domestic utensils
to be filliped with
                  in idyllic
                            hours.
Inferno
      and paradise
                  both his possession,
he sells to old dames
                  whose faculties fail
nail-holes
        from the Cross,
                      the ladder of Ascension,
and feathers
          from the Holy Spirit's
                            tail.

Наконец,
и он
перерос себя,
за него
работает раб.
Лишь наживая,
жря
и спя,
капитализм разбух
и обдряб.
Обдряб
и лег
у истории на пути
в мир,
как в свою кровать.
Его не объехать,
не обойти,
единственный выход –
взорвать!

* * *

Знаю,
лирик
скривится горько,
критик
ринется
хлыстиком выстегать:
– А где ж душа?!
Да это ж –
риторика!
Поэзия где ж? –
Одна публицистика!! –

But finally
          he too
                    outgrew himself
living
     off the blood and sweat
                         of the people.
Just guzzling,
               snoozing
                    and pocketing pelf,
Capitalism
          got lazy and feeble.
All blubber,
          he sprawled
                    in History's way.
No getting over or past him.
So snug
     in his world-wide bed
the one way out
               was to blast him.

                         *   *   *

I know,
     your critics'll
                    grip their whipsticks,
your poets
          will go
               hysteric:
'Call that poetry?
               Sheer publicistics.
No feeling,
          no nothing –
                    just bare rhetoric!'

Капитализм –

                      неизящное слово,
куда изящ ней звучит –

                                  «соловей»,
но я

    возвращусь к нему

                        снова и снова.
Строку

        агитаторским лозунгом взвей.
Я буду писать

            и про то

                   и про это,
но нынче

        не время

                любовных ляс.
Я

  всю свою

               звонкую силу поэта
тебе отдаю,

             атакующий класс.
Пролетариат –

             неуклюже и узко
тому,

      кому

           коммунизм – западня.
Для нас

        это слово –

                  могучая музыка,
могущая

        мертвых

            сражаться поднять.

*   *   *

Sure,
      'Capitalism' rings
                        not so very elegant;
'Nightingale'
              has a far more delicate sound.
Yet I'll go back to it
                    whenever relevant.
Let stanzas
          like fighting slogans resound!
I've never
          been lacking in topics –
                              you know it,
but now's
          no time
                for lovesick tattle.
All
   my thundering power of a poet
is yours,
        my class
                waging rightful battle!
'Proletariat'
            seems
                  too clumsy for using
to those
        whom
              communism throws into a fright.
For us, though,
              it sounds
                      like mighty music
that'll rouse
            the dead
                  to get up and fight.

* * *

Этажи
       уже
          заёжились, дрожа,
клич подвалов
              подымается по этажам:
– Мы прорвемся
           небесам
                  в распахнутую синь.
Мы пройдем
           сквозь каменный колодец.
Будет.
      С этих нар
             рабочий сын –
пролетариатоводец. –
Им
    уже
        земного шара мало.
И рукой,
       отяжелевшей
               от колец,
тянется
       упитанная
             туша капитала
ухватить
       чужой горлец.
Идут,
     железом
          клацая и лацкая.
– Убивайте!
           Двум буржуям тесно! –
Каждое село –
          могила братская,
города́ –
       завод протезный.
Кончилось –
        столы
           накрыли чайные.

Sumptuous
            mansions
                        huddle closer, shivering.
Up their storeys
                goes the cry of basements, quivering:
'We'll break free
                into the sky's
                                wide-open blue,
out
    of the abysmal stone blind alley.
He will come –
                a worker's son all through,
a leader yet unborn,
                    the proletariat to rally.'
Look,
      the world's already small for Capital's ambition;
with his billion-dollar
                    diamond-studded hands,
doomed
        to dream of gain
                        until perdition,
Capital
        goes grabbing other lands.
Off they march,
                in clashing steel,
                                athirst for pillage.
'Kill!'
        they shriek;
                    two moneybags must come to clutches.
Soldiers' graveyards
                    blot out every village,
each town
        becomes a workshop
                            making crutches.
When it's over
            they lay their tables,
                            unfinicky.

Пирогом
        победа на столе.
– Слушайте
           могил чревовещание,
кастаньеты костылей!
Снова
     нас
          увидите
               в военной яви.
Эту
    время
         не простит вину.
Он расплатится,
              придет он
                   и объявит
вам
    и вашинской войне
                войну! –
Вырастают
        на земле
            слезы́ озёра,
слишком
       непролазны
            крови топи.
И клонились
         одиночки фантазеры
над решением
          немыслимых утопий.
Голову
    об жизнь
           разбили филантропы.
Разве
    путь миллионам –
            филантропов тропы?

Victory's
          the cake they carve and share.
But –
      hearken to the burial mounds' ventriloquy,
to the castanets of bones
                    picked clean and bare.
'You will see us once again in
                        war aflare.
Time will not forgive
                  the bloody crime.
He is coming –
            sage and leader –
                          to declare
war on you,
          to end war for all time.'
Lakes of tears
          spread out
                    to flood the globe.
All too deep
          grow blood-mires,
                        all too copious.
Till at last
        lone day-dreamers
                      began to probe
the probabilities
            of fancy-bred utopias.
But –
      philanthropists –
                    they got their brain-pans cracked
against the adamantine rock
                      of actual fact.
How could footpaths
                  blazed by random spurts of brilliance
serve as thoroughfares
                  for all the suffering millions?

И уже
     бессилен
         сам капиталист,
так
  его
     машина размахалась, –
строй его
       несет,
          как пожелтелый лист,
кризисов
       и забастовок хàос.
– В чей карман
       стекаем
           золотою лавой?
С кем идти
      и на кого пенять? –
Класс миллионоглавый
напрягает глаз –
      себя понять.

            *   *   *

Время
    часы
      капитала
        крáло,
побивая
     прожекторов яркость.
Время
    родило
       брата Карла –
старший
     ленинский брат
         Маркс.
Маркс!
   Встает глазам
       седин портретных рама.

Now Capitalism
               himself,
                         the blundering thief,
can't tame them,
               so his cogs' wild tempo rises.
His system's carried
               like a yellow
                         wilted leaf
over the giddy ups and downs
                         of strikes and crises.
What to make
         of all this
                 gold-fed circus,
whom to blame
         and on whose side
                     to stand?
The million-headed,
         million-handed class of workers
strains its brains
         itself to understand.

                  *   *   *

Capital's days
         were eroded
                 and gnarled
by time
     outblazing
             searchlight arcs,
till time
     gave birth
             to a man named Karl –
Lenin's
     elder brother Marx.
Marx!
   His portrait's gray-framed sternness
                         grips one.

Как же

        жизнь его

                от представлений далека!

Люди

        видят

           замурованного в мрамор,

гипсом

        холодеющего старика.

Но когда

          революционной тропкой

первый

        делали

           рабочие

                шажок,

о, какой

        невероятной топкой

сердце Маркс

           и мысль свою зажег!

Будто сам

        в заводе каждом

                стоя сто́ймя,

будто

        каждый труд

              размозоливая лично,

грабящих

        прибавочную стоимость

за руку

        поймал с поличным.

Где дрожали тельцем,

              не вздымая глаз свой

даже

        до пупа

           биржевика-дельца,

Маркс

        повел

          разить

              войною классовой

But what a gulf
            between impressions
                            and his life!
What we see
            immured in marble
                            or in gypsum
seems a cold old man
                    long since past care and strife.
But when the workers took –
                            uncertain yet in earnest –
the first short steps
                    along their revolutionary path,
into what a giant,
                blazing furnace
Marx
    fanned up his mind and heart!
As if he'd drudged whole shifts
                            in every factory
                                        himself
and,
    callousing his hands,
                        each tool and job had handled,
Marx caught
            the pilferers
                        of surplus value
                                    with their pelf,
red-handed.
Where others quailed,
                    eyes dropped too low
                                    in awe
to peer up
        even as high
                    as a profiteer's umbilicus,
Marx
    undertook
            to lead the proletariat
                            into class war

золотого
до быка
дорошего тельца́.
Нам казалось –
в коммунизмовы затоны
только
волны случая
закинут
нас
юля́.
Маркс
раскрыл
истории законы,
пролетариат
поставил у руля.
Книги Маркса
не набора гранки,
не сухие
цифр столбцы –
Маркс
рабочего
поставил на́ ноги
и повел
колоннами
стройнее цифр.
Вел
и говорил: –
сражаясь лягте,
дело –
корректура
выкладкам ума.
Он придет,
придет
великий практик,
поведет
полями битв,
а не бумаг! –

to slay the golden calf,
                by then a bull,
                            immense and bellicose.
Into the bay of communism,
                  still fogged
                        with blinding mystery,
we thought
        the waves of chance alone
                        could bring us
                            from our hell.
Marx
    disclosed the deepest
                  laws of history,
put the proletariat
            at the helm.
No,
   Marx's books
                aren't merely print and paper,
not dust-dry manuscripts
                with dull statistic figures.
His books
      brought order
                  to the straggling ranks of labour
and led them forward,
               full of faith and vigour.
He led them
       and he told them:
                    'Fall in battles!
The proof
       of theories
             are concrete deeds.
He'll come
      one day,
           the genius of practice,
and guide you on
          from books
               to battlefields!'

Жерновами дум
                последнее меля́
и рукой
        дописывая
                      восковой,
знаю,
        Марксу
                виделось
                      видение Кремля
и коммуны
        флаг
                над красною Москвой.

                    *   *   *

Назревали,
        зрели дни,
                    как дыни,
пролетариат
        взрослел
                      и вырос из ребят.
Капиталовы
        отвесные твердыни
валом размывают
                    и дробят.
У каких-нибудь
        годов
                    на расстоянии
сколько гроз
        гудит
                от нарастаний.
Завершается
        восстанием
                    гнева нарастание,
нарастают
        революции
                    за вспышками восстаний.

As he wrote
                his last
                        with fingers trembling,
as the last thoughts
                        flickered in his eyes,
I know,
        Marx
                had a vision
                                of the Kremlin
and the flag
                of the Commune
                                in Moscow's skies.

                        *   *   *

Like melons
                the years came on in maturity.
Labour
        grew out of childhood
                                at length.
Capital's
            bastions
                    lost security
as the proletarian tide
                        gained momentum and strength.
In a matter
            of several years or so
inklings
        of gales
                into tempests grow.
Uprisings
            break out
                    as the climax of wrath,
revolutions
            come
                in their aftermath.

Крут
     буржуев
          озверевший норов.
Тьерами растерзанные,
                воя и стеная,
тени прадедов,
          парижских коммунаров,
и сейчас
       вопят
          парижскою стеною:
– Слушайте, товарищи!
                Смотрите, братья!
Горе одиночкам –
          выучьтесь на нас!
Сообща взрывайте!
           Бейте партией!
Кулаком
     одним
         собрав
             рабочий класс. –
Скажут:
     «Мы вожди»,
          а сами –
               шаркунами?
За речами
       шкуру
           распознать умей!
Будет вождь
       такой,
          что мелочами с нами –
хлеба проще,
       рельс прямей.

               *   *   *

Ruthless
          are the bourgeois' bestial ways;
crushed
          by Thiers' and Galliffet's
                              inhuman hammer,
from Paris,
          from the wall
                    of Père Lachaise
the shadows of the Communards
                              still clamour:
'Look and listen, comrades!
                    Learn from our debâcle!
Woe to single fighters!
                    Let our lesson
                              not be missed.
Only by a party
          can the enemy be tackled,
clenching
          all the working class
                              in one great fist!'
'We are the leaders!'
                    some'll say,
                              then turn about and sting.
Learn to see
          beneath the words:
                              the spotted skin!
There'll be a leader
                    ours
                    to the least thing,
straight as rails, simple as bread,
                    prepared to go through thick and thin.

                    *   *   *

Смесью классов,
            вер,
                  сословий
                        и наречий
на рублях колес
            землища двигалась.
Капитал
      ежом противоречий
рос во-всю
            и креп,
                  штыками иглясь.
Коммунизма
            призрак
                  по Европе рыскал,
уходил
      и вновь
            маячил в отдаленьи...
По всему поэтому
            в глуши Симбирска
родился
      обыкновенный мальчик
                        Ленин.

            *   *   *

Я знал рабочего.
            Он был безграмотный.
Не разжевал
            даже азбуки соль.
Но он слышал,
            как говорил Ленин,
и он
      знал – всё.
Я слышал
      рассказ
            крестьянина-сибирца.

A potpourri
            of faiths and classes,
                            dialects
                                    and conditions,
on wheels of gold
                the great world creaked along.
Capital,
        a very hedgehog of contradictions,
bristling with bayonets,
                        waxed fat and strong.
The spectre
            of Communism
                            haunted Europe,
withdrew, then roamed again
                            throughout its girth.
For all these reasons
                in Simbirsk,
                            half-way from Moscow
                                            to the Urals,
Lenin,
        a boy like any other,
                        came to birth.

                    *   *   *

I knew a worker –
                    he was illiterate –
hadn't even tasted
                    the alphabet's salt,
yet he
        had listened
                    to a speech by Lenin
and so
        knew all.
I remember a story
                    by a Siberian peasant;

Отобрали,
        отстояли винтовками
                и раем
                        разделали селеньице.
Они не читали
              и не слышали Ленина,
но это
      были ленинцы.
Я видел горы –
           на них
                  и куст не рос.
Только
      тучи
            на скалы
                  упали ничком.
И на сто верст
                у единственного горца
лохмотья
         сияли
               ленинским значком.
Скажут –
         это
             о булавках áхи.
Барышни их
              вкалывают
                    из кокетливых причуд.
не булавка вколота –
                 значком
                      прожгло рубахи
сердце,
      полное
             любовью к Ильичу.
Этого
      не объяснишь
              церковными славянскими
                     крюками,

they'd seized land,
               held it
                    and worked it
                           into very heaven.
They'd never even heard,
                   much less read Lenin,
but were Leninists all,
                 from seven to seventy-seven.
I've been up mountains –
                   not a lichen on their sides.
Just clouds
       lying prone
             on a rocky ledge.
The one
     living soul
         for hundreds
             of miles
was a herdsman
         resplendent
             with Lenin's badge.
Some'll call it
       a hankering for pins.
The way girls
       make a frock
            look a bit more rich.
But that pin'll scorch
         through shirts
             and skins,
to the hearts,
       brimful
         of devotion to Ilyich.
This couldn't
       be explained
           by churchmen's
               hooks and crooks;

и не бог
      ему
           велел –
                    избранник будь!
Шагом человеческим,
                    рабочими руками,
собственною головой
                  прошел он
                        этот путь.

*　*　*

Сверху
      взгляд
             на Россию брось –
рассинелась речками,
                    словно
разгулялась
             тысяча розг,
словно
             плетью исполосована.
Но синей,
          чем вода весной,
синяки
         Руси крепостной.
Ты
   с боков
            на Россию глянь –
и куда
         глаза ни кинь,
упираются
            небу в склянь
горы,
       каторги
            и рудники.

no God Almighty
            bade him
                    be a saviour.
Working
        step
            by step
                    his way through life and books,
he grew to be
            the teacher of world labour.

                    *   *   *

Look down
            at Russia
                    from a flying plane.
She's blue
            with rivers
                    as if
lashed all over
            with a willow cane
or striped
            by a seven-tail whip.
But bluer
            than a river
                    ever looks through its rushes
were the bruises
            of landlord-ridden
                            Russia.
Take a sidelong view
                    of the woebegone land:
wherever
            you cast your eyes
mountains,
            pit-heads and prisons stand
propping up
            her skies.

Но и каторг
                больнее была
у фабричных станков
                        кабала.
Были страны
                богатые более,
красивее видал
                        и умней.
Но земли
            с еще большей болью
не довиделось
                видеть
                        мне.
Да, не каждый
                удар
                        сотрешь со щеки.
Крик крепчал:
                – Подымайтесь
                        за землю и волю вы! –
И берутся
                бунтовщики
одиночки
            за бомбу
                        и за револьвер.
Хорошо
        в царя
            вогнать обойму!
Ну, а если
            только пыль
                        взметнешь у колеса?!
Подготовщиком
                цареубийства
                        пойман
брат Ульянова,
                народоволец
                        Александр.

But worse than jail,
                    worse than war in the trenches
was the lot
          of those
                    who slaved at her benches.
There were countries
                    richer by far,
                                   I've heard,
more beautiful,
               more sane,
but never have I met
                    in the whole wide world
a land
      more full
             of sorrow
                       and pain.
Yet pain and contempt
                    can't be borne
                                   forever.
Land and Freedom!
                  the cry grew strong,
until lone rebels,
                  believers
                            in individual terror
took to dynamite,
                 bullet
                       and bomb.
It's well
        to finish
               the tsar at a shot,
but what
        if the bullet
                     goes wide?
And Lenin's brother
                   Alexander
                            is caught
preparing
        regicide.

Одного убьешь –
                другой
                        во весь свой пыл
пытками
        ушедших
                переплюнуть тужится.
И Ульянов
        Александр
                повешен был
тысячным из шлиссельбуржцев.
И тогда
        сказал
                Ильич семнадцатигодовый –
это слово
        крепче клятв
                солдатом поднятой руки:
– Брат,
  мы здесь
        тебя сменить готовы,
победим,
        но мы
                пойдем путем другим! –

                *   *   *

Оглядите памятники –
                видите
                        героев род вы?
Станет Гоголем,
        а ты
                венком его величь.
Не такой –
        чернорабочий,
                ежедневный подвиг
нá плечи себе
        взвалил Ильич.

Shoot a tsar,
          and another
                    with all his might
will strain
        to break
                the record in tortures.
And so
      Alexander Ulyanov
                    one night
was hanged
          by the light of Schlüsselburg torches.
Then his brother,
              a seventeen-year-old youth,
swore an oath
            that was firmer
                        than any.
'Brother,
        we'll take up
                    the battle for truth
and win,
        but by other means,'
                        pledged Lenin.

                    *   *   *

Your usual hero –
                look at the statues –
struts like a peacock:
                    'I'll show you
                                which is which!'
Not such was the feat,
                    arduous,
                            plain,
                                    undramatic,
chosen as the task of his life
                        by Ilyich.

Он вместе,

              учит в кузничной пасти,

как быть,

        чтоб зарплата

                    взросла пятаком.

Что делать,

        если

               дерется мастер.

Как быть,

        чтоб хозяин

                  поил кипятком,

Но не мелочь

          целью в конце:

победив,

        не стой так

над одной

         сметённой лужею.

Социализм – цель.

                  Капитализм – враг.

Не веник –

         винтовка оружие.

Тысячи раз

         одно и то же

он вбивает

        в тугой слух,

а назавтра

         друг в друга вложит

руки

     понявших двух,

Вчера – четыре,

            сегодня – четыреста.

Таимся,

     а завтра

         в открытую встанем,

и эти

    четыреста

        в тысячи вырастут.

Together with men
                from the mills and mines
he sought
        to raise wages
                to a decent level,
looked for ways
            of fighting
                    deductions and fines
and teaching good manners
                    to a foreman-devil.
But the struggle's
                not merely
                    for some such claim –
to sweep up a puddle
                and then go slow –
satisfied
        by a trifle.
Socialism's the aim,
                Capitalism the foe
and the weapon
            no broom but a rifle.
The same things
            again
                and again
                    and again
he hammers down
            into the work-dimmed brain.
And tomorrow
            those who've at last
                        understood
pass it on,
        making the lesson good.
Yesterday it was dozens,
                    today it's hundreds,
tomorrow
        thousands
                into action rising,

Трудящихся мира
                подымем восстанием.
Мы уже
        не тише вод,
                    травинок ниже –
гнев
    у трудящихся
                густится в туче.
Режет
    молниями
                Ильичевых книжек.
Сыпет
        градом
                прокламаций и летучек,
Бился
        об Ленина
                темный класс,
тёк
    от него
            в просветленьи,
и, обданный
            силой
                и мыслями масс,
с классом
            рос
                Ленин.
И уже
        превращается в быль
    то,
        в чем юношей
                    Ленин клялся:
– Мы
        не одиночки,
                    мы –
                            союз борьбы
за освобождение
                рабочего класса. –

till the whole working world
                              will start rumbling like thunder
and break
          into an open uprising.
We're no longer timid
                    as newly-born lambkins;
the workers' wrath
                  condenses
                              into clouds,
slashed
        by the lightning
                        of Lenin's pamphlets,
his leaflets
          showering
                    on surging crowds.
The class
        drank its fill
                      of Lenin's light
and, enlightened,
                  broke
                        from the gloom of millennia.
And in turn,
            imbibing
                    the masses' might,
together with the class
                      grew Lenin.
And gradually,
            enriched
                      by the fertile communion,
they bring
          young Vladimir's pledge
                                  to realisation,
no longer
          each on his own,
                          but a Union of Fighters
for Working Class
                  Emancipation.

Ленинизм идет
          все далее
               и более
вширь
      учениками
           Ильичевой выверки.
Кровью
      вписан
           героизм подполья
в пыль
      и в слякоть
             бесконечной Володимирки.
Нынче
     нами
         шар земной заверчен.
Даже
    мы,
       в кремлевских креслах если, –
скольким
      вдруг
         из-за декретов Нерчинск
кандалами
       раззвонится в кресле!
Вам
   опять
       напомню птичий путь я.
За волчком –
        трамваев
             электрическая рысь.
Кто
   из вас
      решетчатые прутья
не царапал
       и не грыз?!

Leninism spreads
                    ever wider
                                and deeper.
Lenin's disciples
                    work miracle after miracle,
the underground's grit
                    traced in blood-drops
                                        seeping
through the dust
                    and slush
of the endless
                    Vladimirka.
Today
        we spin
                the old globe our way.
Yet even
        when debating
                        in Kremlin armchairs
there's few
            won't suddenly recall a day
filled
        with the groans
                        of chain-gang marchers.
Remember
            the none-too-distant past:
beyond the eye-hole,
                    trams, droshkies,
                                        cars…
Who
        of you,
                let me ask,
didn't bite
            and tear
                    at prison-bars?

Лоб
      разбей
            о камень стенки тесной –
за тобою
            смыли камеру
                  и замели.
«Служил ты недолго, но честно
на благо родимой земли».
Полюбилась Ленину
                  в какой из ссылок
этой песни
      траурная сила?

* * *

Говорили –
      мужичок
            своей пойдет дорогой,
заведет
      социализм
            бесхитростен и прост.
Нет,
   и Русь
      от труб
            становится сторóгой.
Город
   дымной бородой оброс.
Не попросят в рай –
            пожалуйста,
                  войдите –
через труп буржуазии
                  коммунизма шаг.
Ста крестьянским миллионам
                  пролетариат водитель.
Ленин –
      пролетариев вожак.

We could smash out
                    our brains
                                on the walls weighing on us:
All they did was mop up
                    and strew sand.
'It wasn't long but honest,
                    Your service to your land…'
In which of his exiles
                    did Lenin
                                get fond
of the mournful power
                    of that song?

                    *   *   *

The peasant –
                    'twas urged –
                                would blaze his own tracks
and set up socialism
                    without hitch or wrangle.
But no –
        Russia too
                    goes bristling with stacks;
black beards of smoke
                    round her cities tangle.
There's no god
            to bake us
                    pies in the skies.
The proletariat
            must head
                    the peasant masses.
Over capital's corpse
                    Russia's highroad
                                    lies,
with Lenin
        to lead the toiling classes.

Понаобещает либерал
                    или эсерик прыткий,
сам охочий до рабочих шей, –
Ленин
        фразочки
                с него
                        пооборвет до нитки,
чтоб из книг
            сиял
                в дворянском нагише.
И нам
        уже
            не разговорцы досужие,
что-де свобода,
                что люди братья, –
мы
    в марксовом всеоружии
одна
        на мир
            большевистская партия.
Америку
        пересекаешь
                    в экспрессном купе,
идешь Чухломой –
                    тебе
в глаза
        вонзается теперь
                    Р К П
и в скобках
            маленькое «Б».
Теперь
        на Марсов
                охотится Пулково,
перебирая
        небесный ларчик.

They'd promise heaps,
                    wordy liberals and S.R.s,
themselves not loath
                    to saddle workers' backs.
Lenin made
          short work of their yarns,
left them bare
              as babies
                        in the blaze of facts.
He soon disposed
                 of their empty prattle
full of 'liberty',
                'fraternity'
                          and suchlike words.
Arming
      with Marxism,
                    mustering for battle,
rose the only
          Bolshevik Party
                          in the world.
Now,
     touring the States
                      in a de luxe coupe,
or footing it through Russia –
                          wherever you be
they meet you,
              the letters
                       R.C.P.
with their bracketed neighbour,
                              B.
Today
     it's red Mars
                    astronomers are hunting,
telescopes
          scanning the sky from a high tower.

Но миру
     эта
        строчная буква
в сто крат красней,
             грандиозней
                 и ярче.

*   *   *

Слова
     у нас
        до важного самого
в привычку входят,
            ветшают, как платье.
Хочу
     сиять заставить заново
величественнейшее слово
            «ПАРТИЯ».
Единица! –
        Кому она нужна?!
Голос единицы
        оньше писка.
Кто ее услышит? –
        Разве жена!
И то
     если не на базаре,
        а близко.
Партия –
     это
        единый ураган,
из голосов спрессованный
            тихих и тонких,
от него
     лопаются
        укрепления врага,
как в канонаду
        от пушек
            перепонки.

Yet that modest letter
                on paper
                        or bunting
shines to the world
                ten times redder
                        and brighter.

*   *   *

Words –
        even the finest –
                        turn into litter,
wearing threadbare
                with use and barter.
Today
        I want to infuse new glitter
into the most glorious of words:
                        PARTY.
Individual –
            what can he mean in life?
His voice sounds fainter
                        than a needle dropping.
Who hears him?
            Only, perhaps,
                        his wife,
and then if she's near
                and not working or shopping.
A Party's
        a raging,
                single-voiced storm
compressed
        out of voices
                        weak and thin.
The enemy strongholds
                        burst with its roar
like eardrums
            when cannon
                    begin their din.

Плохо человеку,
                когда он один.
Горе одному,
                один не воин –
каждый дюжий
                ему господин,
и даже слабые,
                если двое.
А если
        в партию
                сгру́дились малые –
сдайся, враг,
                замри
                        и ляг!
Партия –
        рука миллионопалая,
сжатая
        в один
                громящий кулак.
Единица – вздор,
                единица – ноль,
один –
        даже если
                очень важный –
не подымет
                простое
                        пятивершковое бревно,
тем более
        дом пятиэтажный.
Партия –
        это
                миллионов плечи,
друг к другу
        прижатые туго.

One man alone
                feels down and out.
One man alone
                won't make weather.
Any old bully
            can knock him about –
even weaklings
                if two together.
But when
        we midgets
                    in a Party stand –
surrender,
        enemy,
                fade
                    out of sight!
A Party's
        a million-fingered hand
clenched
        into one fist
                    of shattering might.
What's an individual?
                    No earthly good.
One man,
            even the most important of all,
can't raise a ten-yard log of wood,
to say nothing
                of a house
                            ten stories tall.
A Party means millions
                    of arms,
                            brains,
                                    eyes
linked
        and acting together.

Партией
      стройки
          в небо взмечем,
держа
    и вздымая друг друга.
Партия –
      спинной хребет рабочего класса.
Партия –
      бессмертие нашего дела.
Партия – единственное,
           что мне не изменит.
Сегодня приказчик,
      а завтра
           царства стираю в карте я.
Мозг класса,
     дело класса,
         сила класса,
             слава класса –
           вот что такое партия.
Партия и Ленин –
      близнецы-братья –
кто более
     матери-истории ценен?
Мы говорим Ленин,
       подразумеваем –
           партия,
мы говорим
     партия,
       подразумеваем –
          Ленин.

*   *   *

In a Party
        we'll rear our projects to the skies,
upholding and helping
                one another.
The Party's
        the compass that keeps us on course,
the backbone
            of the whole working class.
The Party
        embodies the immortality of our cause,
our faith
        that will never
                    fail or pass.
Yesterday an underling,
                today whole empires I'm uncharting.
The brain,
    the strength,
            the glory of its class,
                        that's what it is,
                                our Party.
Lenin and the Party
                are brother-twins.
Who'll say which means more
                    to History – their mother?
Lenin
    and the Party
                are the closest kin;
name one
        and you can't but imply
                        the other.

*   *   *

Еще
     горой
          коронованные гла́вы,
и буржуи
       чернеют
              как вороны в зиме,
но уже
     горение
           рабочей лавы
по кратеру партии
              рвется из-под земель.
Девятое января.
          Конец гапонщины.
Падаем,
     царским свинцом косимы.
Бредня
     о милости царской
               прикончена
с бойней Мукденской,
          с треском Цусимы.
Довольно!
     Не верим
          разговорам посторонним!
Сами
   с оружием
          встали пресненцы.
Казалось –
     сейчас
          покончим с троном,
за ним
   и буржуево
         кресло треснется.

Crowns and coronets
                    still galore,
bourgeois
         still blacken
                    like wintering crows.
But labour's lava
              already starts to pour:
see –
     through the Party's crater
                              it flows.
January 9.
          Gapon,
                 the 'people's friend',
debunked.
           We fall
                 in the rifles' crackle.
Tall tales
         about the tsar's royal mercy
                                     end
with Mukden's bloodbath
                       and Tsushima's debâcle.
Enough!
         No belief left
                       for twaddle and twiddle.
The Presnya
            takes to arms,
                         done with ballyhoo.
It seemed
         the throne
                    would soon snap across the middle
and forthwith
          the bourgeois easy chair too.

Ильич уже здесь.

        Он изо дня на́ день

проводит

        с рабочими

                пятый год.

Он рядом

        на каждой стоит баррикаде,

ведет

        всего восстания ход.

Но скоро

        прошла

           лукавая вестийка –

«свобода».

          Бантики люди надели,

царь

        на балкон

            выходил с манифестиком.

А после

        «свободной»

           медовой недели

речи,

        банты

          и пения плавные

пушечный рев

          покрывает басом:

по крови рабочей

            пустился в плавание

царев адмирал,

          каратель Дубасов.

Плюнем в лицо

        той белой слякоти,

сюсюкающей

        о зверствах Чека!

Смотрите,

        как здесь,

            связавши за́ локти,

рабочих на́смерть

        секли по щекам.

Ilyich is everywhere.
                    Day after day
he fights
          with the workers
                              through 1905,
standing nearby
                    on every barricade,
innerving
            the revolution with his vigour and drive.
But soon
          came the treacherous trick:
                                        Hey Presto!
Red ribbons
              blossomed like a virgin's cheek.
The tsar
        from his balcony
                            read the Manifesto.
Then,
      after a 'free'
                      honey-week,
the speeches,
              the singing,
                              the hooraying and hailing
are covered
            by the treble bass of
cannon:
        on the workers' blood goes sailing
the tsar's butcher-admiral
                            Dubasov.
Spit in the faces
                    of white dross who tell us
about the Cheka's
                    blood-dousings!
They ought to have seen
                          how, tied by the elbows,
workers
        were flogged to death
                                by thousands.

Зверела реакция.
                    Интеллигентчики
ушли от всего
                    и всё изгадили.
Заперлись дома,
                    достали свечки,
ладан курят –
                    богоискатели.
Сам заскулил
                    товарищ Плеханов:
– Ваша вина,
                    запутали, братцы!
Вот и пустили
                    крови лохани!
Нечего
        зря
            за оружье браться. –
Ленин
        в этот скулеж недужный
врезал голос
                    бодрый и зычный:
– Нет,
        за оружие
                    браться нужно,
только более
                    решительно и энергично.
Новых восстаний вижу день я.
Снова подымется
                    рабочий класс.
Не защита –
                    нападение
стать должно
                    лозунгом масс. –
И этот год
        в кровавой пене

Reaction ran amuck.
                    Intellectual bunglers
withdrew, recluses,
                    and became the meekest,
locked themselves in
                    with blinking candles
and smoked incense,
                    god-damn God-seekers.
Even Comrade Plekhanov himself
                              raised a whine:
'It's the Bolsheviks' fault;
                    theirs was the muddle.
Shouldn't have taken up arms
                         at the time
and blood wouldn't swirl,
                    as it does now,
                              in puddles.'
But here
     with his courage
                    never failing
Lenin
    cut
        into the traitors' wail:
'O yes we should have –
                    I'll repeat it daily –
only far more resolutely –
                    and wouldn't have failed.
I see
     the hour of new upheavals
arriving again
          to bring out
                    the working classes.
Not defence but attack
               should become the masses' driving slogan.'
That nightmare year
                with the bloody bath

и эти раны
            в рабочем стане
покажутс
            школой
                    первой ступени
в грозе и буре
                грядущих восстаний.

*   *   *

И Ленин
        снова
              в своем изгнании
готовит
        нас
            перед новой битвой,
Он учит
        и сам вбирает знание,
он партию
          вновь
             собирает разбитую.
Смотри –
        забастовки
               вздымают год,
еще –
        и к восстанию сумеешь сдвинуться ты.
Но вот
        из лет
           подымается
               страшный четырнадцатый.
Так пишут –
        солдат-де
             раскурит трубку,
балакать пойдет
        о походах древних,
но эту
        всемирнейшую мясорубку
к какой приравнять

and the massacre
                of the workers' insurgent millions
will pass
       and appear
               as preparatory class
for the hurricanes
             of future rebellions.

*　*　*

And Lenin
        once more
               turns exile into college,
educating us
          for the coming battle,
teaching others,
             himself gaining knowledge,
regathering the Party,
               unmanned and scattered.
Year after year
           the strikes scored higher:
a spark
      and the people would
                  flare up again.
But then
       came a year
              that put off the fire –
1914
     with its deluge of pain.
It's thrilling
          when veterans
                 twirl their whiskers
and, smirking,
           spin yams
              about old campaigns.
But this wholesale,
            world-wide
                   auction of mincemeat –

к Полтаве,
                    к Плевне?!
Империализм
            во всем оголении -

живот наружу,
            с вставными зубами,
и море крови
            ему по колени –
сжирает страны,
            вздымая штыками.
Вокруг него
            его подхалимы –
патриоты –
            приспособились Вовы –
пишут,
        руки предавшие вымыв:
– Рабочий,
        дерись
            до последней крови! –
Земля –
        горой
            железного лома,
а в ней
        человечья
            рвань и рваль,
Среди
        всего сумасшедшего дома
трезвый
        встал
            один Циммервальд.
Отсюда
        Ленин
            с горсточкой товарищей
встал над миром
            и поднял над

with what Poltava
          or Plevna
                will it compare?
Imperialism
      in all
        his filth and mud,
false teeth bared,
          growling and grunting,
quite at home
       in the gurgling ocean of blood,
went swallowing up
           country after country.
Around him,
      cosy,
         social-patriots and sycophants,
raising heavenwards
         the hands
           that betray,
scream like monkeys
         till everyone's sick of it:
'Worker –
     fight on –
        on with the fray!'
The world's
      iron scrap-heap
          kept piling and piling,
mixed with minced man's-flesh
          and splintered bone.
In the midst
      of all this
        lunatic asylum
Zimmerwald
       stood sober alone.
Ever remembered
         is the speech Lenin made
              above the world uproar

мысли
      ярче
            всякого пожарища,
голос
      громче
            всех канонад.
Оттуда –
      миллионы
                  канонадою в уши,
стотысячесабельной
                  конницы бег,
отсюда,
      против
            и сабель и пушек, –
скуластый
      и лысый
            один человек.
– Солдаты!
      Буржуи,
            предав и продав,
к туркам шлют,
      за Верден,
                  на Двину.
Довольно!
      Превратим
            войну народов
в гражданскую войну!
Довольно
      разгромов,
            смертей и ран,
у наций
      нет
            никакой вины.
Против
      буржуазии всех стран
подымем
      знамя
            гражданской войны! –

raising on high
              a voice
                    far louder
                             than any cannonade,
thoughts more inflaming
                   than any fire.
On one side
         were millions
                    writhing in the labour
of war
      to bring would-be victory
                         forth,
on the other –
            against both cannon and sabre –
one man
        of ordinary
                stature and girth.
'Soldiers!
        The bourgeois
                 betray and sell you,
send you to slaughter
                 as a thousand times before.
Enough of it!
         Hear what I tell you:
Turn this war
         among nations
                   into civil war.
What are we,
        peoples,
               arguing for?
Put an end
        to catastrophes,
                  wounds
                     and losses.
Raise the banner
           of holy war
against
      the world-wide bosses!

Думалось:
       сразу
              пушка-печка
чихнет огнем
              и сдунет гнилью,
потом поди,
              ищи человечка,
поди,
       вспоминай его фамилию.
Глоткой орудий,
              шипевших и вывших,
друг другу
       страны
              орут –
                     на колени!
Додрались,
       и вот
              никаких победивших –
один победил
       товарищ Ленин.
Империализма прорва!
Мы
   истощили
              терпенье ангельское.
Ты
   восставшею
                     Россией прорвана
от Тавриза
       и до Архангельска.
Империя –
       это тебе не ку̀ра!
Клювастый орел
              с двухглавою властью.
А мы,
   как докуренный окурок,
просто
   сплюнули
              их династью.

It looked as though,
                    infernally booming,
the cannon would sneeze
                          and blow him away.
Who'd ever find
              the fragile human?
Who would remember
                  his name?
'Surrender!'
          one country roared to another.
Looked as if they'd go on fighting
                            for millennia.
But at last it was over,
                  and lo,
                          no winners
except for one –
              Comrade Lenin.
Imperialism,
          damn you!
You've exhausted our patience,
                          once fit for angels.
Rebellious
        Russia
              has rammed you
through –
        from Tebriz to Archangel.
An empire's no hen –
                  no joke bagging it,
the two-headed,
              power-vested,
                          hook-beaked eagle.
And yet
      we spat out
                like a finished fag-end
their dynasty
          with all trappings,
                        regal and legal.

Огромный,
          покрытый кровавою ржою,
народ,
          голодный и голоштанный,
к Советам пойдет
                или будет буржую
таскать,
          как и встарь,
                    из огня каштаны?
– Народ
          разорвал
                    оковы царьи,
Россия в буре,
               Россия в грозе, –
читал
     Владимир Ильич
                    в Швейцарии,
дрожа,
       волнуясь
                над кипой газет.
Но что
       по газетным узнаешь клочьям?
На аэроплане
               прорваться б ввысь,
туда,
      на помощь к восставшим рабочим, –
одно желанье,
               единая мысль.
Поехал,
        покорный партийной воле,
в немецком вагоне,
                  немецкая пломба.
О, если бы
          Знал тогда Гогенцоллерн,
что Ленин
          и в их монархию бомба!

                    *   *   *

The nation
            scrambling out of the mire,
huge,
      famished,
                  blood-crust all over it –
would it go on
                  dragging chestnuts from the fire
for the bourgeois,
                  or would it go Soviet?
'The people
            have broken
                        tsarist fetters.
Russia's boiling,
                  Russia's ablaze!'
Lenin read
            in newspapers and letters
in Switzerland
            where he lived those days.
But what could one fish
                        out of newsprint tatters?
Oh, for an airplane
                  skyward to speed –
home,
      to the aid
                  of the workers in battle –
that was his only longing and need.
But at last
            at the Party's bidding
                              he is on wheels.
If only
      the murderous Hohenzollern knew
that the German goods waggon
                              under German seals
carried a bomb
            for his monarchy, too!

                  *   *   *

Питерцы
              всё еще
                        всем на радость
лобзались,
                   скакали детишками малыми,
но в красной ленточке,
                              слегка припарадясь,
Невский
         уже
              кишел генералами.
За шагом шаг –
                   и дойдут до точки,
дойдут
         и до полицейского свиста.
Уже
    начинают
              казать ноготочки
уржуи
         из лапок своих пушистых.
Сначала мелочь –
                   вроде мальков́.
Потом повзрослее –
                        от шпротов до килечек.
Потом Дарданельский,
                        в девичестве Милюков,
за ним
       с коронацией
                        прет Михаильчик,
Премьер
       не власть –
                        вышивание гладью!
Это
    тебе
         не грубый нарком.
Прямо девушка –
                   иди и гладь её!
Истерики закатывает,
                   поет тенорком.

Petrograd citizens
                    still kept skipping,
exulting
       in glee ephemeral.
But already,
          red-ribboned,
                  in martial frippery,
the Nevsky swarmed
             with treacherous generals.
Another few months
             and they'll reach the limit:
it'll come
       to policemen's whistles.
The bourgeois
         already itch to begin it,
already
     the fur
          on the beast's back bristles.
At first
    mere fry
        at which one might scoff,
then big sharks
        emerged
           to swallow
                the nation.
Next Dardanelsky,
          née Milyukov,
and finally
      Prince Mikhail
           agog for coronation.
The Premier
        wields power
               with feathery splendour:
none of your commissar's snarling.
Sings
   in a tenor
        maidenly tender,

Еще
     не попало
          нам
               и росинки
   от этих самых
             февральских свобод,
а у оборонцев –
          уже хворостинки –
«марш, марш на фронт,
               рабочий народ».
И в довершение
          пейзажа славненького,
нас предававшие
          и до
            и пото́м,
вокруг
     сторожами
            эсеры да Савинковы,
меньшевики –
       ученым котом.
И в город,
     уже
        заплывающий салом,
вдруг оттуда,
       из-за Невы,
с Финляндского вокзала
по Выборгской
         загрохотал броневик.
И снова
     ветер
       свежий, крепкий
валы
   революции
        поднял в пене.
Литейный
     залили
       блузы и кепки.

even kicks up hysterics,
                    the darling.
We hadn't yet tasted
                    the sorriest crumbs
of February's
            freedom-prodigies
when
    'Off to the front,
                    working thingumajigs!'
the war-boys
            began prodding us.
And to crown
            this picture
                        of passing beauty,
traitors and doublecrossers
                        before and after that,
S.R.s and Savinkovs
                stood on watchdog duty
with Mensheviks
                as the Tell-Tale Cat.
When suddenly
            into the city
                        sleekening with blubber,
from beyond
            the broad-banked Neva,
from Finland Station
through the Vyborg suburb
                        rumbled an armoured car.
And again
        the gale,
                momentum gaining,
set
    the whirlwind
                of revolution spinning.
Caps and blouses
                flooded
                        the Liteyny:

«Ленин с нами!
                    Да здравствует Ленин!»
–Товарищи! –
            и над головами
                            первых сотен
вперед
        ведущую
                    руку выставил. –
– Сбросим
            эсдечества
                        обветшавшие лохмотья.
Долой
        власть
                соглашателей и капиталистов!
Мы –
        голос
                воли низа,
рабочего низа
                всего света.
Да здравствует
                партия,
                        строящая коммунизм,
да здравствует
                восстание
                            за власть Советов! –
Впервые
        перед толпой обалделой
здесь же,
        перед тобою,
                        близ,
встало,
        как простое
                    делаемое дело,
недосягаемое слово –
                    «социализм».

'Lenin's with us!
                    Long live Lenin!'
'Comrades',
            and over the heads
                            of the hundreds clapping
forward
        a guiding hand
                    he thrust,
'Let's cast off
            the outworn Social-Democrat
                                    trappings.
Chuck the capitalists
                    and their yes-men
                                    into the dust!
We voice
        the will
                of the toilers
                            and tillers
of the whole world.
                    Now's the hour.
Long live the Party
                of communism builders,
long live
        armed struggle
                    for Soviet power!'
For the first time ever
                    without ado
before the flabbergasted
                    human ocean
arose
    as a routine job to do
once unattainable
                socialism.

Здесь же,
            из-за заводов гудящих,
сияя горизонтом
                во весь свод,
встала
        завтрашняя
                    коммуна трудящихся –
без буржуев,
            без пролетариев,
                            без рабов и господ.
На толщь
        окрутивших
                    соглашательских веревок
слова Ильича
            ударами топора.
И речь
        прерывало
                обвалами рева:
«Правильно, Ленин!
                Верно!
                        Пора!»
Дом
    Кшесинской,
                за дрыгоножество
подаренный,
            нынче –
                    рабочая блузница.
Сюда течет
            фабричное множество,
здесь
    закаляется
                в ленинской кузнице.
«Ешь ананасы,
            рябчиков жуй,
день твой последний
                приходит, буржуй».

There,
     beyond the factories roaring,
there, on the horizon
               with blinding force
it shone
     before us,
          the Commune
               of tomorrow
without bourgeois,
          proletarians,
               slaves
                    or lords.
Through the tangle
          of tethering
              yes-men's tenets
Lenin's speech
          came crashing like an axe,
indented with uproar
          every minute:
'Right,
     Lenin!
        It's time to act!
Kshesinskaya's palace,
             earned by twiddling toes
today is invaded
        by boots
            steel-heeled.
It's here
     the factory multitude flows
 in Lenin's smithy
        to be tempered
              and steeled.
'Munch your pineapples,
           chew your grouse!
Your days are over,
         bourgeois louse!'

Уж лезет
        к сидящим
                в хозяйском стуле –
как живете
        да что жуете?
Примериваясь,
        в июле
за горло потрогали
                и за животик.
Буржуевы зубья
                ощерились разом.
– Раб взбунтовался!
                Плетями,
                        да в кровь его! –
И ручку
        Керенского
                водят приказом –
на мушку Ленина!
                В Кресты Зиновьева!
И партия
        снова
                ушла в подполье.
Ильич на Разливе,
                Ильич в Финляндии.
Но ни чердак,
        ни шалаш,
                ни поле
вождя
        не дадут
                озверелой банде их.
Ленина не видно,
                но он близ.
По тому,
        работа движется как,
видна
        направляющая
                ленинская мысль,

Already
        we demanded
                        the wherefore and why
from those
        who, lording it,
                        quaffed and guzzled,
and during
        the dress rehearsal of July
tickled their gizzards
                        with revolver muzzles.
The bosses bared fangs,
                        their looks spelt murder:
'Rioting slaves!
        We'll show 'em!'
                        they thundered.
'Lenin to the wall!'
                Kerensky penned the order;
'To jail with Zinoviev!'
                and the Party
                        went underground.
Ilyich is in Finland,
                at Razliv,
                        safe and sound,
hidden securely
                in a twig shelter.
It won't betray him
                to the pack of hounds
ready
    to snap him up
                in the welter.
Lenin's unseen,
                and yet he's near,
and time and events
                don't stand.
Every slogan
        is Lenin's idea,

видна
      ведущая
            ленинская рука.
Словам Ильичевым –
                 лучшая почва:
падают,
      сейчас же
            дело растя,
и рядом
      уже
         с плечом рабочего –
плечи
      миллионов крестьян.
И когда
      осталось
            на баррикады выйти,
день
   наметив
       в ряду недель,
Ленин
     сам
       явился в Питер:
– Товарищи,
         довольно тянуть канитель!
Гнет капитала,
           голод-уродина,
войн бандитизм,
              интервенция во́рья –
будет! –
     покажутся
            белее родинок
на теле бабушки,
       древней истории. –

every move
        is guided
                by Lenin's hand.
Each word
        by Ilyich
                finds soil most fertile
and falling
        forthwith
                promotes
                        our cause,
and see –
        alongside
                with Leninist workers
millions of peasants
                into its orbit it draws.
And when
        it remained
                but to mount barricades,
having chosen
        a day out of many,
back to Petrograd
                to the workers' aid
with 'Comrades,
        we've waited enough!'
                        came Lenin.
'The yoke of capital,
                hunger's prodding,
the banditry of wars
                and thieving intervention
will seem
        in time
                mere moles on the body
of Grandma History,
                escaping attention.'

И оттуда,
        на дни
                оглядываясь эти,
голову
      Ленина
             взвидишь сперва.
Это
    от рабства
              десяти тысячелетий
к векам
        коммуны
                  сияющий перевал.
Пройдут
        года
              сегодняшних тягот,
летом коммуны
                согреет летá,
и счастье
        сластью
               огромных ягод
дозреет
        на красных
                  октябрьских цветах.
И тогда
        у читающих
                ленинские веления,
пожелтевших
          декретов
                  перебирая листки,
 выступят
        слезы,
             выведенные из употребления,
и кровь
        волнением
                ударит в виски.

And looking back
    from the future
       on this day
the first thing
   seen
    will be Lenin's figure,
from millennia
   of slavery
     blazing the way
to the age of the Commune
     through want
       and rigour.
These years
   of privation
     will sink into the past
and the summer
   of the Commune
      warm this globe of ours,
and the huge,
   sweet fruit of happiness
      at last
will mature
  from the crimson
     October flowers.
And then
  the readers
    of Lenin's behests,
as the yellowing pages
    they peruse,
will feel a hot tide
   well up in their breasts,
and in their eyes –
   hot tears,
     long since out of use.

Когда я
         итожу
                 то, что про́жил,
и роюсь в днях –
                 ярчайший где,
я вспоминаю
                 одно и то же –
двадцать пятое,
                 первый день.
Штыками
         тычется
                 чирканье молний,
матросы
         в бомбы
                 играют, как в мячики.
От гуда
         дрожит
                 взбудораженный Смольный.
В патронных лентах
                 внизу пулеметчики.
– Вас
         вызывает
                 товарищ Сталин.
Направо
         третья,
                 он
                         там. –
– Товарищи,
         не останавливаться!
                         Чего стали?
В броневики
         и на почтамт! –
– По приказу
         товарища Троцкого! –

When I look
          for the grandest day
                         of my life,
rummaging
          in all
               I've gone through and seen,
I name without doubt
                    or internal strife
October 25,
          1917.
The Smolny throbs
                    in a buzz of excitement.
Grenades
       hang on seamen
                    like partridges.
Bayonets zigzag
               like flashes of lightning.
Below stand
          machine-gunners
                         belted with cartridges.
No aimless shuffling
                    in the corridors;
with bombs
          and rifles
                    no one's a novice.
'Comrade Stalin
               wants to see you.
Here
    are the orders:
armoured cars –
               to the General Post Office.'
'Comrade Trotsky's
                    instructions.'

– Есть! –
                повернулся
                        и скрылся скоро,
и только
        на ленте
                у флотского
под лампой
        блеснуло –
                «Аврора».
Кто мчит с приказом,
                        кто в куче споря
кто щелкал
        затвором
                на левом колене.
Сюда
        с того конца коридорища
бочком
        пошел
                незаметный Ленин.
Уже
        Ильичем
                поведенные в битвы,
еще
        не зная
                его по портретам,
толкались,
        орали,
                острее бритвы
солдаты друг друга
                крыли при этом.
И в этой желанной
                железной буре
Ильич,
        как будто
                даже заспанный,

'Right!'
        – he dashed forward
and the man's
                navy ribbons
                        flashed:
                                'Aurora'
Some run with dispatches,
                others
                        stand arguing,
still others
        click rifle-bolts –
                        no two figures the same.
And here,
        no token
                of greatness
                        or grandeur,
brisk
    but inconspicuous,
                Lenin
                        came.
Already
    led by Lenin
                into battle,
they didn't know him
                from portraits
                        yet;
bustled,
        hollered,
                exchanged banter,
with a quickfire of oaths,
                        hail-fellow-well-met.
And there, in that long-wished-for
                        iron storm
Lenin,
    drowsy with fatigue,
                it would seem,

шагал,

      становился

            и глаз, сощуря,

вонзал,

      заложивши

            руки зá спину.

В какого-то парня

      в обмотках,

              лохматого,

уставил

      без промаха бьющий глаз,

как будто

      сердце

           с-под слов выматывал,

как будто

      душу

          тащил из-под фраз.

И знал я,

      что всё

          раскрыто и понято

и этим

      глазом

          наверное выловится –

и крик крестьянский,

             и вопли фронта,

и воля нобельца,

         и воля путиловца.

Он

  в черепе

        сотней губерний ворочал,

людей

      носил

          до миллиардов полутора,

Он

  взвешивал

        мир

          в течение ночи,

pacing,
        stopping,
                hands clasped behind back,
dug his eyes
        into the motley scene.
Once I saw him
            stabbing them
                    into a chap in puttees,
dead-aiming,
        sharp-edged
                as razors,
seizing the gist
            as pincers would seize,
dragging the soul
            from under words and phrases.
And I knew,
        everything
                was disclosed
                        and understood,
everything
        those eyes
                were raking for:
where
    the shipwright
                and miner stood,
what
    the peasant and soldier were aching for.
He
    kept all races
                within his sight,
all continents
        where the sun goes setting
                            or dawning;
weighed the whole globe
                in his brain
                        by night

а утром:
– Всем!

      Всем!

           Всем это –
фронтам,

          кровью пьяным,
рабам

      всякого рода,
в рабство

         богатым отданным.
Власть Советам!
Земля крестьянам!
Мир народам!
Хлеб голодным!
Буржуи

      прочли

         – погодите,

                 выловим. –
животики пятят

        доводом веским –
ужо им покажут

         Духонин с Корниловым,
покажут ужо им

         Гучков с Керенским.
Но фронт

      без боя

         слова эти взяли –
деревня

      и город

         декретами залит,
и даже

     безграмотным

           сердце прожег.
Мы знаем,

     не нам,

        а им показали,
какое такое бывает

       «ужо».

and in the morning:
'To all,
        every
                and each,
slaves of the rich
                one another
                                hacking and carving;
to you we appeal
                this hour:
Let the Soviets
                take over government power!
Bread to the starving!
Land to the farmers!
Peace to the peoples
and their warring armies!'
The bourgeois,
                busy
                        drinking their fill of
soldierly blood,
                shrieked in a frenzy:
'At 'em,
        Dukhonin and Kornilov,
show 'em what's what,
                        Guchkov and Kerensky!'
But both front and rear
                        surrendered without a shot
when the decrees
                hailed down on them,
                                        scorching.
Today we know
                who showed whom
                                what's what;
even at illiterates' hearts
                        they got,
into steel determination
                        forging.

Переходило
                от близких к ближним,
от ближних
                дальним взрывало сердца:
«Мир хижинам,
война,
        война,
               война дворцам!»
Дрались
        в любом заводе и цехе,
горохом
        из городов вытряхали,
                       а сзади
шаганье октябрьское
                метило вехи
пылающих
        дворянских усадеб.
Земля –
        подстилка под ихними порками,
и вдруг
        ее,
             как хлебища в узел,
со всеми ручьями ее
                  и пригорками
крестьянин взял
             и зажал, закорузел.
В очах
        манжетщики,
                злобой похаркав,
ползли туда,
            где царство да графство.
Дорожка скатертью!
                Мы и кухарку
каждую
        выучим
            управлять государством!

* * *

From near
            unto far it went rolling,
mounting
            from a whisper to a roar:
'Peace to cottages poor and lowly,
war on palaces,
                war, war,
                        war!'
We fought
            in all factories, humble and famous,
shook 'em out of cities like peas,
                        while outside
the October wildfire
                left flaming manors
for landmarks
            marking
                    its triumphant stride.
The land –
            once a mat for wholesale floggings –
was suddenly seized
                    by a calloused hand –
with rivulets,
            hillocks
                    and other belongings
and held tight –
            the long-dreamed-of,
                        blood-soaked land.
The spectacled white-collars,
                        spitting in spite,
sneaked off
            to where kingdoms and dukedoms
                            still remain.
Good riddance!
            We'll train every cook so she might
manage the country
                to the workers' gain.

                    *   *   *

Мы жили
            пока
                        производством ротаций.
С окопов
            летело
                        в немецкие уши:
– Пора кончать!
                        Выходите брататься! –
И фронт
            расползался
                        в улитки теплушек.
Такую ли
            течь
                        загородите горстью?
Казалось –
                        наша лодчонка кренится –
Вильгельмов сапог,
                        Николаева шпористей,
сотрет
            Советской страны границы.
 Пошли эсеры
                        в плащах распашонкой,
ловили бегущих
                        в свое словоблудьище,
тащили
            по-рыцарски
                        глупой шпажонкой
красиво
            сразить
                        броневые чудища!
Ильич
            петушившимся
                        крикнул:
                                    – Ни с места!
Пусть партия
            взвалит
                        и это бремя.

We survived
      for the time
            by printing,
                 writing,
bellowing
     from the trenches
            into the German ear:
'Come out and fraternise!
            Finish fighting!
Enough!'
     and the front
            crumbled off into the rear.
Leaking in torrents
           that swelled out of trickles,
it seemed
     our boat was about to careen:
Wilhelm's boot,
        far heftier than Nicholas's,
would smash the country
           to smithereens.
Then came the S.R.s
          with their infantile drivelling,
to catch the runners
         in their word-traps preposterous;
dragged them back
      with toy swords
             from the scrap-heap
                 of chivalry
picturesquely to vanquish
         the iron-clad monsters.
But Lenin
     curbed
       the gamecocks' zest:
'The Party
     must shoulder
        the burden again.

Возьмем
        передышку похабного Бреста.
Потеря – пространство,
                выигрыш – время. –
Чтоб не передо́хнуть
            нам
                в передышку,
чтоб знал –
запомнят уда́ры мои,
себя
    не муштровкой –
                сознанием вышколи,
стройся
        рядами
            Красной Армии.

                        *   *   *

Историки
        с гидрой плакаты выдерут
– чи эта гидра была,
                чи нет? –
а мы
    знавали
            вот эту гидру
в её
    натуральной величине.
«Мы смело в бой пойдем
            за власть Советов
            и как один умрем
            в борьбе за это!»
        Деникин идет.
            Деникина выкинут,
обрушенный пушкой
                подымут очаг.
Тут Врангель вам –
            на смену Деникину.

We'll accept
               the breathing-space of filthy Brest:
Territory we'll lose,
                  but time we'll gain.'
And, so
        as the breathing-space
                           shouldn't kill us,
to be able,
          later,
               to knock them barmy,
let discipline
          and conscious resolve
                           be our drillers.
Rally
     in the ranks
               of the Red Army!

                    *   *   *

Historians
          will stare at the posters with hydras:
'Did those hydras
                  exist or not?'
As for us,
        that same hydra
                         reached out to bite us
and a full-size hydra it was, by god.
          'All dangers we'll defy,
          No limit to our courage,
          And fighting we will die
          For Soviet power to flourish!'
First comes Denikin.
                    Denikin gets a lickin'.
Repair work begins
                 on our ruined hearths.
Then Wrangel turns up
                    in the wake of Denikin;

Барона уронят –
                уже Колчак.
Мы жрали кору,
                ночевка – болотце,
но шли
        миллионами красных звезд,
и в каждом – Ильич,
                и о каждом заботится
на фронте
        в одиннадцать тысяч верст.
Одиннадцать тысяч верст
                    окружность,
а сколько
        вдоль да поперек!
Ведь каждый дом
                атаковывать нужно,
каждый
    врага
        в подворотнях берег.
Эсер с монархистом
                шпионят бессонно –
где жалят змеей,
                где рубят с плеча.
Ты знаешь
        путь
            на завод Михельсона?
Найдешь
        по крови
            из ран Ильича.
Эсеры
    целят
        не очень верно –
другим концом
            да себя же
                в бровь.

the baron kicked out,
                    Kolchak comes en masse.
Our dinners – bark,
                    bed – any-old-where,
yet forward
            the red-starred legion bursts.
In each lives Lenin,
                    each feels Lenin's care,
each along a front
                    of eleven thousand versts.
That was its breadth –
                    eleven thousand versts,
but who knows
            its depth and length?
Every door
            an enemy ambush nursed,
every house
            to be captured
                        took blood and strength.
S.R.s and monarchists
                    with their tongues and guns
sting,
      the vipers,
                or bite like hounds.
You don't know the way
                    to Michelson's?
You'll find it
            by the blood
                        from Lenin's wounds.
S.R.s
      talk better
                than they pull a trigger,
their bullets
            their own ribs ramming.

Но бомб страшнее
                    и пуль револьве́рных
осада голода,
            осада тифо́в.
Смотрите –
        кружат
               над крошками мушки,
сытней им,
        чем нам
               в осьмнадцатом году, –
простаивали
            из-за осьмушки
сутки
      в улице
          на холоду.
Хотите сажайте,
           хотите травите –
завод за картошку –
               кому он не жалок!
И десятикорпусный
            судостроитель
пыхтел
       и визжал
           из-за зажигалок.
А у кулаков
          и масло и пышки.
Расчет кулаков
           простой и верненький -
запрячь хлеба́
          да зарой в кубышки
николаевки
         да ке́ренки.

But a menace beside which
                              bullets were meagre
was the siege begun by typhus
                              and famine.
Look at the crumb-collecting
                              flies:
by far
      better off
                  than we were then,
queueing
        in the freeze
                        for a tiny slice
days
    on end.
Fancy
      a giant shipbuilding works
working for nothing
                    but cigarette-lighters!
Jail 'em,
        hang 'em,
                  cut their heads off,
how else
        could the workers earn grub,
                                      poor blighters?
But the kulaks
              had heaps of both butter and flour.
Kulaks,
       they weren't no boobies;
hid and hoarded
               till a fitter hour
their grain
          and their greasy rubles.

Мы знаем –
       голод
            сметает начисто,
тут нужен зажим,
               а не ласковость воска,
и Ленин
        встает
             сражаться с кулачеством
и продотрядами
              и продразверсткой.
Разве
      в этакое время
             слово «демократ»
набредет
        какой головке дурьей?!
Если бить,
        так чтоб под ним
               панель была мокра:
ключ побед –
        в железной диктатуре.

                 *   *   *

Мы победили,
        но мы
            в пробоинах:
 машина стала,
        обшивка –
            лохмотья.
Валы обломков!
          Лохмотьев обойных!
Идите залейте!
        Возьмите и смойте!

Hunger
        hits harder,
                    kills surer than bullets.
You need a steel grip here,
                    not cotton-wool lenience.
So Lenin
        sets out
                to fight the kulaks
by food requisition teams –
                    grim expedients.
How could the very notion
                    of democracy
at such a time
            enter
                any fool's head?!
At 'em
        and none of your mincing hypocrisy.
Only iron dictatorship
                to victory led.

*   *   *

We've won,
            but our
                    ship's all dents and holes,
hull in splinters,
                engines near end,
overhaul overdue
                for floors,
                        ceilings,
                            walls.
Come, hammer and rivet,
                    repair and mend!

Где порт?
          Маяки
                    поломались в порту,
кренимся,
          мачтами
                    волны крестя!
Нас опрокинет –
                    на правом борту
в сто миллионов
                    груз крестьян.
В восторге враги
                    заливаются воя,
но так
          лишь Ильич умел и мог –
он вдруг
          повернул
                    колесо рулевое
сразу
          на двадцать румбов вбок.
И сразу тишь,
                    дивящая даже;
крестьяне
          подвозят
                    к пристани хлеб.
Обычные вывески
                    – купля –
                              – продажа –
– нэп.
     Прищурился Ленин:
                              Чинитесь пока чего,
аршину учись,
                    не научишься –
                              плох. –
Команду
          усталую
                    берег покачивал.
Мы к буре привыкли,
                    что за подвох?

Where's port? –
                    all the beacons
                                    gone dead in the harbour.
We careen,
            crossing
                        the waves with our masts.
There's risk she'll keel over,
                                such cargo to starboard:
the 100 million
                    peasant class!
While enemies howled
                        with malicious glee
Lenin alone
            kept his nerve:
turned her twenty points leeward
                                    and she
swerved upright
                and entered port at a curve.
And at once,
            surprisingly,
                            no more gale;
peasants cart bread
                    and at every step
the familiar ads:
                    WILL BUY –
                                    FOR SALE –
– NEP
Lenin winks:
            we're in for repairs.
Get used to the yardstick –
                            nothing to fear.
The shore
            rocks the crew,
                            weak with wear and tear:
'Whoah!
        Where's the gale?
                            What's the big idea?'

Залив
      Ильичем
             указан глубокий
и точка
      смычки-причала
             найдена,
и плавно
      в мир,
           строительству в доки,
вошла
      Советских республик громадина.
И Ленин
      сам
         где железо,
             где дерево
носил
      чинить
         пробитое место.
Стальными листами
          вздымал
             и примеривал
кооперативы,
      лавки
         и тресты.
И снова
      становится
           Ленин штурман,
огни по бортам,
         впереди и сзади.
Теперь
      от абордажей и штурма
мы
   перейдем
         к трудовой осаде.
Мы
   отошли,
      рассчитавши точно.

Lenin
    points out
           a deep bay free of rocks
with the piers
      of co-operatives
              looming over it.
And smoothly
      into construction's
             docks
sailed
    the colossal country of Soviets.
Lenin
    himself
      heaves timber and iron
to patch up
     the breaks and ruptures,
marks off and measures
        with an all-seeing eye on
future co-ops,
     shops
       and management structures.
Then again
     he resumes
       his post on the bridge:
Lights on
    in front,
      at the sides
        and back!
Since now,
     systematic
       everyday
         siege
will replace
     both storm raid
       and surprise attack.
At first
    we withdrew,
       discreet and sober.

Кто разложился –
                на берег
                        за во́рот.
Теперь вперед!
                Отступленье окончено.
РКП,
        команду на борт!
Коммуна – столетия,
                        что десять лет для ней?
Вперед –
        и в прошлом
                        скроется нэпчик.
Мы двинемся
                во сто раз медленней,
зато
    в миллион
                прочней и крепче.
Вот этой
        мелкобуржуазной стихии
еще
    колышется
                мертвая зыбь,
но тихие
        тучи
            молнией выев,
уже –
    нарастанье
                всемирной грозы.
Враг
    сменяет
            врага поределого,
но будет –
            над миром
                    зажжем небеса

Anyone disgraced –
                out
                    without a word!
Now forward again –
                    the retreat is over.
R.C.P. –
        crew aboard!
The Commune'll live centuries.
                            What's a decade for her?
Forward,
        and this quagmire of an NEP
                            will be past.
We'll move and build
                    a hundred times slower
so
    a million times longer
                        our edifice may last.
The morass
            of petty 'private enterprise'
still tethers
            the tempo
                    of our advance,
but through the gathering clouds
                            of the world-wide tempest
the first streaks of lightning
                        already
                            glance.
Old enemies drop
                and give place to new.
Yet wait –
            the skies
                    over the world
                            we'll ignite.

– но это
            уже
                  полезней проделывать,
чем
      об этом писать. –
Теперь,
        если пьете
                    и если едите,
на общий завод ли
                    идем
                          с обеда,
мы знаем –
            пролетариат – победитель,
и Ленин –
            организатор победы.
От Коминтерна
                до звонких копеек,
серпом и молотом
                    в новой меди,
одна
      неписаная эпопея –
шагов Ильича
              от победы к победе.
Революции –
              тяжелые вещи,
один не подымешь –
                    согнется нога.
Но Ленин
          меж равными
                        был первейший
по силе воли,
              ума рычагам.
Подымаются страны
                    одна за одной –
рука Ильича
            указывала верно:

But that
          is surely
                    better
                         to do
than simply to write about. Right?
Today,
          whether in the office
                              of a director
or running a lathe
                    at a public-owned
                                        factory,
we know –
            the proletariat is victor,
and Lenin
          the architect of victory.
From the Comintern
                    to the hammer and sickle
on brand-new kopeks
                    shining in glory,
our achievements
                    and triumphs
                                double
                                     and triple,
filling page after page
                    of Lenin's great story.
Revolutions
          are the business of peoples;
for individuals
                they're too heavy to wield,
yet Lenin
          ranked foremost
                         among his equals
by his mind's momentum,
                         his will's firm steel.
Countries rise
               one after the other,
fulfilling
          his predictions each in turn:

народы –
        черный,
            белый
                и цветной –
становятся
          под знамя Коминтерна.
Столпов империализма
                    непреклонные колонны –
буржуи
        пяти частей света,
вежливо
        приподымая
               цилиндры и короны,
кланяются
          Ильичевой республике советов.
Нам
    не страшно
            усилие ничье,
мчим
    вперед
          паровозом труда..
и вдруг
      стопудовая весть –
                с Ильичем
удар.

*　*　*

Если бы
        выставить в музее
плачущего большевика,
весь день бы
        в музее
             торчали ротозеи.
Еще бы –
      такое
          не увидишь и в века!

men of all races –
                white
                      and dark-skinned –
rally
     under the banner
                   of the Comintern.
The imperialists
                and bourgeois
                             in their bossy crowds,
still pestering the world
                       and lording over it,
politely tip
          their top hats and crowns
to llyich's brain-child –
                        the Republic of Soviets.
Fearing
       no effort
                 or artifice by the rich,
on speeds our engine
                    in curling smoke.
When suddenly –
                the shattering news:
                                   Ilyich
had a stroke...

                        *   *   *

If
   you exhibited
                in a museum
a Bolshevik in tears,
all day
       they'd flock to the museum
                                  to see him.
Small wonder –
               you won't
                         see the like in years.

Пятиконечные звезды
              выжигали на наших спинах
                            панские воеводы.
Живьем,
        по голову в землю,
                      закапывали нас банды
                                  Мамонтова.
В паровозных топках
              сжигали нас японцы,
рот заливали свинцом и оловом,
отрекитесь! – ревели,
                но из
горящих глоток
              лишь три слова:
– Да здравствует коммунизм! –
Кресло за креслом,
                ряд в ряд
эта сталь,
        железо это
вваливалось
          двадцать второго января
в пятиэтажное здание
                  Съезда советов.
Усаживались,
          кидались усмешкою,
решали
      походя
            мелочь дел.
Пора открывать!
                Чего они мешкают?
Чего
    президиум,
              как вырубленный, поредел?
Отчего
      глаза
          краснее ложи?
Что с Калининым?
                Держится еле.

With five-pointed stars
                    we were branded
                                    by Polish *voivodes*.
Buried alive
            neck-deep in the ground
                                by the bandits of
                                                Mamontov,
burned up in engine fire-boxes
                                by Japanese marauders,
mouths plugged with molten tin,
                                threatened with bullets;
'Renounce it!' they bellowed,
                            but from
the hell-holes of burning gullets
'Long live Communism!'
                            was all that would come.
Row after row,
            in its might unreckoned,
this iron,
        this steel,
                    the recess not over yet,
crowded
        on January the twenty-second
the five-storey building
                        of the Congress of Soviets.
Down they settled,
                joking
                        and grinning,
affairs talked over
                in business-like idiom.
Time to start!
            Why aren't they beginning?
Here,
    what are those gaps in the presidium?
Why are their eyes
                    red as box-stall plush?
Look at Kalinin –
                hardly keeps his feet.

Несчастье?

      Какое?

           Быть не может!

А если с ним?

      Нет!

           Неужели?

Потолок

      на нас

           пошел снижаться вороном.

Опустили головы –

         еще нагни!

Задрожали вдруг

         и стали черными

люстр расплывшихся огни.

Захлебнулся

         колокольчика ненужный щелк.

Превозмог себя

        и встал Калинин.

Слёзы не сжуешь

        с усов и щек.

Выдали.

      Блестят у бороды на клине.

Мысли смешались,

         голову мнут.

Кровь в виски,

       клокочет в вене:

– Вчера

     в шесть часов пятьдесят минут

скончался товарищ Ленин! –

              * * *

Something happened?
                        What is it?..
                                Hush!
What if it's him?
                No, indeed…
Raven-like
        the ceiling swooped upon us,
                                        lowering;
down dropped heads,
                bent floorward by their fears.
Of a sudden
        ghastly,
                blackly glowering
grew the swimming lights
                        of chandeliers.
Silence choked the bell's unneeded tinkle.
Up Kalinin got,
                by will alone.
Tears – won't be chewed up
                        by moustache and wrinkle:
they betray him,
                shining
                        on the beard's sharp cone.
Veins ablaze –
                no hope of quenching them;
thoughts confused –
                like walls his head impending;
'Yesterday
        at 6.50 p.m.
died Comrade Lenin.'

*   *   *

Этот год
        видал,
                чего не взвидят сто.
День
    векам
        войдет
            в тоскливое преданье.
Ужас
    из железа
           выжал стон.
По большевикам
            прошло рыданье.
Тяжесть страшная!
              Самих себя же
                    выволакивали
                        волоком.
Разузнать –
        когда и как?
               Чего таят!
В улицы
    и в переулки
            катафалком
плыл
    Большой театр.
Радость
      ползет улиткой.
У горя
      бешеный бег.
Ни солнца,
        ни льдины слитка –
всё
   сквозь газетное ситко
черный
      засеял снег.
На рабочего
        у станка
весть набросилась.
           Пулей в уме.

That year
        beheld a sight
                        that ages won't set eye on.
That day
      will keep
              its tale of woe
                            forever throbbing.
Horror
      squeezed an anguished groan
                              from iron.
The rows of Bolsheviks
                    were swept with waves of sobbing.
What a weight!
            We dragged
                      ourselves out bodily.
Get the details!
              When and where?
                            Why do they hide it,
                                        damn!
Through the streets and lanes,
                          a white hearse modelling,
the Bolshoi Theatre swam.
Joy
    crawls on like a snail.
Grief
    will never go slow.
No sun shone.
            No ice
                gleamed pale.
All the world
            from the newspapers' pail
was cold-showered
                  with coal-black snow.
On the worker
            bent at his gears
the news pounced
                and bullet-like burned.

И как будто
                слезы́ стакан
опрокинули на инструмент.
И мужичонко,
                видавший виды,
смерти
        в глаз
                смотревший не раз,
отвернулся от баб,
                но выдала
кулаком
        растертая грязь.
Были люди – кремень,
                и эти
прикусились,
        губу уродуя.
Стариками
        рассерьезничались дети,
и, как дети,
        плакали седобородые.
Ветер
    всей земле
                бессонницею выл,
и никак
    восставшей
                не додумать до конца,
что вот гроб
        в морозной
                комнаточке Москвы
революции
        и сына и отца.
Конец,
    конец,
            конец.
                    Кого
уверять!
        Стекло –
            и видите под…

And it seemed
                a cupful of tears
on his instruments overturned.
And the peasant,
                weathered and wizened by life,
whom death
        more than once
                        just missed,
swung round –
                away from his wife,
but she saw it –
                the dirt he smudged with his fist.
There were some –
                    no flint could be harder or colder,
yet they too
        clenched their teeth,
                        lips awry.
Children
        in a minute grew graver and older
and, childlike,
                the grey-bearded started to cry.
The wind
        to all the earth
                        in sleepless anguish whined,
and she, the rebel,
                couldn't stand up to the notion
that here, in Moscow,
                    in a frosty room enshrined
lay he –
        both son and father
                        of the Revolution.
The end,
        the end,
                the end…
                        All persuasion
useless!
        Glass
                and beneath – the deceased.

Это
    его
        несут с Павелецкого
по городу,
            взятому им у господ.
Улица,
     будто рана сквозная –
так болит
      и стонет так.
Здесь
    каждый камень
          Ленина знает
по топоту
       первых
            октябрьских атак.
Здесь
    всё,
      что каждое знамя
              вышило,
задумано им
      и велено им.
Здесь
    каждая башня
         Ленина слышала,
за ним
    пошла бы
        в огонь и в дым.
Здесь
    Ленина
       знает
         каждый рабочий,
сердца́ ему
      ветками елок стели.
Он в битву вёл,
       победу пророчил,
и вот
    пролетарий –
        всего властелин.

It's him
        they bear
                    from Paveletsky Station
through the city
                    that he from the lords released.
The street's like a wound
                            that'll worsen and worsen,
so the ache of it
                    cuts and hacks.
Here every cobble
                    knew Lenin
                                in person
by the tramp
            of the first
                        October attacks.
Here
    every slogan
                on banners embroidered
was thought out
                and worded
                            by him.
Here every tower
                his speeches
                            applauded,
would follow him
                anywhere,
                            staunch and grim.
Here Lenin
            is known
                        both in works and offices.
Spread hearts
            like spruce-tree boughs
                                    in his way!
He led,
        he steeled with his victory-prophecies,
and see –
            proletarians
                        have taken sway.

Здесь
        каждый крестьянин
                    Ленина имя
в сердце
        вписал
                любовней, чем в святцы.
Он зѐмли
        велел
                назвать своими,
что дедам
        в гробах,
                засеченным, снятся.
И коммунары
            с-под площади Красной,
казалось,
        шепчут:
                – Любимый и милый!
Живи,
    и не надо
                судьбы прекрасней –
сто раз сразимся
                и ляжем в могилы! –
Сейчас
        прозвучали б
                    слова чудотворца,
чтоб нам умереть
                и его разбудят, –
плотина улиц
            враспашку раство́рится,
и с песней
        на́ смерть
                    ринутся люди.
Но нету чудес,
            и мечтать о них нечего.
Есть Ленин,
        гроб
            и согнутые плечи.

Here every peasant
                    holds Lenin's name
dearer
        than any
                of kinsmen cherished
for the land
            that at Lenin's bidding became
his own –
            a dream
                    for which grandsires rebelled
                                            and perished.
And Communards
                    from their graves
                                    in Red Square
seemed to be whispering
                        'Dear,
                                beloved,
live,
        and no need
                    for a lot more fair.
We'd die ten times
                    for fulfilment of it.'
Let the word
            be pronounced
                            by a miracle-maker
for us to die
            that he be awoken;
the street-streams would swell
                                and flood their embankments
and all
        go to death
                    with a joy unspoken.
But there aren't any miracles.
                            Only Lenin.
Lenin,
        his coffin
                and our bent shoulders.

Он был человек
                    до конца человечьего –
неси
        и казнись
                    тоской человечьей.
Вовек
        такого
                    бесценного груза
еще
        не несли
                    океаны наши,
как гроб этот красный,
                            к Дому союзов
плывущий
                на спинах рыданий и маршей.
Еще
        в караул
                    вставала в почетный
суровая гвардия
                        ленинской выправки,
а люди
        уже
                прожидают, впечатаны
во всю длину
                и Тверской
                            и Димитровки.
В семнадцатом
                было –
                        в очередь дочери
за хлебом не вышлешь –
                            завтра съем!
Но в эту
        холодную,
                    страшную очередь
с детьми и с больными
                        встали все.

This man was a human –
                        as human as anyone.
So just bear it –
            the pain
                        that in humans smoulders.
Never
    was there
                a burden more precious
borne along
            by oceans of people
than this red coffin
                    borne by processions
on the drooping shoulders
                        of marches and weeping.
The Guard of Honour
                    had scarcely been formed
of heroes,
        heirs
                of his wisdom and strength,
when crowds,
            impatient,
                    already swarmed
through all the neighbourhood's
                                breadth
                                    and length.
Into a 1917 breadline
no hunger
            could drive –
                        better eat tomorrow.
But into this bitter,
                freezing,
                        dread line
kids,
    invalids –
                all
                    were driven by sorrow.

Деревни

        строились

                с городом рядом.

То мужеством горе,

                то детскими вызвенит.

Земля труда

            проходила парадом –

живым

        итогом

                ленинской жизни.

Желтое солнце,

             косое и лаковое,

взойдет,

           лучами к подножью кидается.

Как будто

          забитые,

               надежду оплакивая,

склоняясь в горе,

              проходят китайцы.

Вплывали

        ночи

            на спинах дней,

часы меняя,

          путая даты.

Как будто

        не ночь

            и не звезды на ней,

а плачут

        над Лениным

              негры из Штатов.

Мороз небывалый

             жарил подошвы.

А люди

      днюют

          давкою тесной.

Alongside
            village and town
                        were arrayed,
child and adult,
            wrung by their grief's insistence.
The world of labour
                passed
                        in parade,
the living
        total
            of Lenin's existence.
Downcast, the sunbeams
                    dropped through the trees,
slanting down
            from the house-top slopes,
pallid
    as whipped-into-meekness Chinese
bent with their sorrow,
                lamenting their hopes.
Nights
    swam in
            on the shoulders
                        of days
muddling hours
            and confusing dates
and it seemed,
            not night
                    with its star-born rays,
but Negroes were here
                with their tears
                            from the States.
The frost, unheard-of,
                scorched one's feet,
yet days
        were spent
                in the tightening crush.

Даже
            от холода
                        бить в ладоши
никто не решается –
                        нельзя,
                                    неуместно.
Мороз хватает
            и тащит,
                        как будто
пытает,
            насколько в любви закаленные.
Врывается в толпы.
                        В давку запутан,
вступает
            вместе с толпой за колонны.
Ступени растут,
                        разрастаются в риф.
  но вот
            затихает
                        дыханье и пенье,
и страшно ступить –
                        под ногою обрыв –
бездонный обрыв
                        в четыре ступени.
Обрыв
        от рабства в сто поколений,
где знают
            лишь золота звонкий резон.
Обрыв
        и край –
                    это гроб и Ленин,
а дальше –
            коммуна
                    во весь горизонт.

Nobody
     even ventures
           to beat
hands together to warm them –
               hush!
The frost grips fast and tortures,
             as if
trying how tough
         the love-tempered will is,
cuts into mobs,
      and, freezing them stiff,
sneaks in
     with the crowds
           behind the pillars.
The steps expand,
        grow up into a reef.
Silence.
     Breathing and sighing stop:
how pass it,
      fearful beyond belief,
that dismal, abysmal
        four-step drop?
That drop
     from the logic of farthing and penny,
from ages
    of thraldom to His Majesty Gold;
that drop
     with its brink –
         the coffin
            and Lenin
and beyond –
      the Commune
          in its glory unrolled

Что увидишь?!
        Только лоб его лишь,
и Надежда Константиновна
             в тумане
                  за…
Может быть,
      в глаза без слез
               увидеть можно больше.
Не в такие
       я
        смотрел глаза.
Знамен
       плывущих
            склоняется шелк
последней
       почестью отданной:
«Прощай же, товарищ,
            ты честно прошел
свой доблестный путь, благородный».
Страх.
     Закрой глаза
          и не гляди –
как будто
      идешь
         по проволоке прóвода.
Как будто
      минуту
         один на один
остался
     с огромной
         единственной правдой.

* * *

Lenin's forehead
                    was all you saw
and Nadezhda Konstantinovna
                         in a haze…
Maybe
      eyes less full of tears
                          could show me more.
It's through clearer eyes
                     I've looked on gladder days.
The floating banners
                 bend
                      in the last
honours,
        and, silken, sway.
'Farewell to you,
              comrade,
                      who have passed
from a noble life
               away…'
Horror!
      Shut your eyes
                   and blindfold pace
the infinity
          of tight-rope grief.
As if
     for a minute
                 left face to face
with the only
            truth
                 worth belief.

*   *   *

Я счастлив.

        Звенящего марша вода

относит

      тело мое невесомое.

Я знаю –

      отныне

           и навсегда

во мне

      минута

          эта вот самая.

Я счастлив,

      что я

         этой силы частица,

что общие

      даже слезы из глаз.

Сильнее

    и чище

        нельзя причаститься

великому чувству

        по имени –

            класс!

Знамённые

    снова

        склоняются крылья,

чтоб завтра

    опять

        подняться в бой –

«Мы сами, родимый, закрыли

орлиные очи твои».

Только б не упасть,

        к плечу плечо,

флаги вычернив

        и ве́ками алея,

на последнее

        прощанье с Ильичем

шли

   и медлили у мавзолея.

What joy!
      My body,
                light as a feather,
drifts
    in the march-tune's resonant stream.
I know
      for sure –
             from now and forever
the light of this minute
             in me will gleam.
What a joy
        it is
          to be part of this union,
even tears from the eyes
             to be shared en masse,
in this –
     the purest,
           most potent communion
with that glorious feeling
          whose name is
                Class.
The banner-wings
        droop
          one after another,
in tomorrow's battle
        again to rise;
'We ourselves, dear brother,
closed your eagle eyes…'
Shoulder to shoulder –
         not to fall!
Flags blackened,
       eyes reddening,
            tears agleam,
for the last farewell with Lenin
         came all,
slowing down
     at the Mausoleum.

Выполняют церемониал.
Говорили речи.
                Говорят – и ладно.
Горе вот,
          что срок минуты
                        мал –
разве
      весь
            охватишь ненаглядный!
Пройдут
        и на̀верх
                  смотрят с опаской,
на черный,
            посыпанный снегом кружок.
Как бешено
          скачут
                  стрелки на Спасской.
В минуту –
          к последней четверке прыжок.
Замрите
        минуту
                от этой вести!
Остановись,
            движенье и жизнь!
Поднявшие молот,
                стыньте на месте.
Земля, замри,
            ложись и лежи!
Безмолвие.
            Путь величайший окончен.
Стреляли из пушки,
                а может, из тыщи.
И эта
      пальба
            казалась не громче,
чем мелочь,
            в кармане бренчащая –
                          в нищем.

On went the funeral ceremonial.
Speeches flowed.
                    Ay, speaking's all right;
the tragedy is
                there's a minute only –
how embrace him
                    at one insatiable sight!
Out they file
                and with dread in their glance
look up
        at the glowering,
                            snow-pocked disk:
how madly
            the clockhands on Spasskaya dance!
A minute –
            and past the last quarter
                                    they whisk!
Stop
    at this news,
                mankind,
                        and grow dumb.
Life,
    movement,
                breathing – cease.
You,
    with hammer uplifted,
                            be numb.
Earth,
        lie low
                and, motionless, freeze.
Silence.
        The end of the greatest of fighters.
Cannon fired.
                A thousand, perhaps.
Yet all that cannonade
                        sounded quieter
than pennies
            jingling in beggars' caps.

До боли
          раскрыв
                    убогое зрение,
почти заморожен,
                    стою не дыша.
Встает
          предо мной
                    у знамён в озарении
тёмный
          земной
                    неподвижный шар.
Над миром гроб,
                    неподвижен и нем.
У гроба
          мы,
                людей представители,
чтоб бурей восстаний,
                          дел и поэм
размножить то,
                    что сегодня видели.

                    *   *   *

Но вот
          издалёка,
                    оттуда,
                          из алого
в мороз,
          в караул умолкнувший наш,
чей-то голос –
                как будто Муралова –
«Шагом марш».
Этого приказа
                и не нужно даже –
реже,
      ровнее,
            тверже дыша,

Straining,
          paining
                    each puny iris
I stand,
        half-frozen,
                      with
                            bated breath.
In the gleaming of banners
                            before me arises
darkling,
          the globe,
                      as still as death.
And on it –
            this coffin
                        mourned by mankind,
with us,
        mankind's representatives,
                                  round it,
in a tempest of deeds
                      and uprisings destined
to build up
            and complete
                          all this day has founded.

                    *   *   *

But now,
        from the bowing banners'
                                red arch
comes the voice
                of Muralov:
'Forward march!'
The command's so apt
                    it needn't be given:
our breathing firmer,
                      more even
                            and rare,

с трудом
        отрывая
                тело-тяжесть,
с площади
        вниз
              вбиваем шаг.
Каждое знамя
              твердыми руками
вновь
        над головою
                взвито ввысь.
Топота потоп,
           сила кругами,
ширясь,
        расходится
              миру в мысль.
Общая мысль
            воедино созвеньена
рабочих,
        крестьян
              и солдат-рубак:
– Трудно
        будет
              республике без Ленина.
Надо заменить его –
             кем?
                И как?
Довольно
        валяться
              на перине, клоповой!
Товарищ секретарь!
           Ná тебе –
                вот –
просим приписать
          к ячейке еркаповой
сразу,
        коллективно,
              весь завод... –

leaden bodies
          with effort
                    driven,
we hammer
          our footsteps
                    down from the square.
Each of the banners
                    above our heads
in steadying hands
                    soars up
                         as it ought.
From our marching ranks
                    the energy spreads
in circles,
          carrying through the world
                              one thought;
one thought
          from a common anxiety
                              stemming
burns
     in the army,
                    at the lathe,
                              at the plough:
it'll be
     hard
          for the Republic without Lenin.
He's got to be replaced,
                    but by whom
                              and how?
'Enough of dozing
               on bug-ridden mattresses!
Comrade secretary,
                    here's
                         our application:
put down
          the whole of the factory
on the membership list
                    of the Party organisation.'

Смотрят
        буржуи,
                глазки раскоряча,
дрожат
        от топота крепких ног.
Четыреста тысяч
                от станка
                        горячих –
Ленину
        первый
                партийный венок.
– Товарищ секретарь,
                        бери ручку…
Говорят – заменим…
                Надо, мол…
Я уже стар –
        берите внучика,
не отстает –
        подай комсомол. –

                    *   *   *

Подшефный флот,
                подымай якоря,
в море
        пора
                подводным кротам.
«По морям,
        по морям,
нынче здесь,
                завтра там».
Выше, солнце!
                Будешь свидетель –
скорей
        разглаживай траур утра.

Cold sweat
        comes oozing
                    from bourgeois flesh
as they watch on,
            grinding their teeth.
400,000
        from the workbench
                        fresh –
could the Party
            bring Lenin
                    a welcomer wreath?
'Comrade secretary,
                where's your pen?
Replace means replace –
                    why squander words?
If you think I'm too old,
                    here's my grandson then;
From the Komsomol –
                one of the early birds!

                    *   *   *

Ahoy, my Navy,
                get into motion!
Off on your missions,
                    submarine moles!
'Over sea
        and over ocean
travel sailors,
            merry souls!'
Hi there, Sun,
            come and be witness!
Hurry on,
        smooth out the wrinkles of mourning.

В ногу
     взрослым
                 вступают дети –
тра́-та-та-та́-та
            та́-та-та-та́.
«Раз,
     два,
          три!
Пионеры мы.
Мы фашистов не боимся,
                 пойдем на штыки».
Напрасно
        кулак Европы задран.
Кроем их грохотом.
              Назад!
                 Не сметь!
Стала
     величайшим
              коммунистом-организатором
даже
     сама
         Ильичева смерть.
Уже
     над трубами
              чудовищной рощи,
руки
     миллионов
            сложив в древко,
красным знаменем
              Красная площадь
вверх
     вздымается
         страшным рывком.

In line
        with parents,
                        children show their fitness –
Tra-ta-ta-ta-ta
                ta-ta-ta-ta!
sing their bugles in the morning.
'One
        two
                three,
Pioneers are we:
We aren't afraid of fascists –
                                Let them come and see!'
In vain
        old Europe
                        snarls like a cur.
'Back!'
        we warn her,
                        'better be wiser!'
Lenin's
        very death
                        has turned
into the greatest
                        communist-organiser!
Over the world-wide forest
                                of factory
                                        stacks
like a giant banner
                the huge
                        Red Square,
millions
        of hands
                welded into its staff,
soars
        with a mighty sweep
                        into the air.

С этого знамени,
              с каждой складки
снова
      живой
            взывает Ленин:
– Пролетарии,
              стройтесь
                        к последней схватке!
Рабы,
      разгибайте
                спины и колени!
Армия пролетариев
                  встань стройна!
Да здравствует революция,
                          радостная и скорая!
Это –
      единственная
                    великая война
из всех,
        какие знала история.

[1924]

And from that banner,
                    from every fold
Lenin,
      alive as ever,
                    cries:
'Workers,
          prepare
                    for the last assault!
Slaves,
        unbend
                your knees and spines!
Proletarian army,
                    rise in force!
Long live the Revolution
                        with speedy victory,
the greatest
            and justest
                        of all the wars
ever fought
            in history!'

[1924]

Notes

p35, Felix Dzerzhinsky (1877-1926) was chairman of the Cheka (All-Russia Extraordinary Commission for Combatting Counter-Revolution and Sabotage) established in December 1917 to defend the gains of the Revolution.

p43, the Hall of Columns was the main hall in the House of Unions, where Lenin's body lay in state in January 1924.

p45, Bromley's and Gujon's were large steelworks in pre-revolutionary Moscow.

p49, GG Yeliseyev was a big food dealer with shops in Moscow and Petersburg.

p53, Ivanovo-Voznesensk (now Ivanovo) was textile city, one of the major centres of revolutionary activity in Russia.

p53, Stepan Razin was the leader of a seventeenth-century peasant uprising.

p77, Adolph Thiers, was the French Premier who in 1871 crushed the Paris Commune.

p87, AI Ulyanov (1866-1887) was Lenin's brother, arrested for participating in an attempt on the life of Tsar Alexander III, and in 1887 executed in Schlüsselburg Fortress.

p91, the Union of Fighters for Working Class Emancipation was the name of the revolutionary organisation founded by Lenin in 1895.

p93, the Vladimirka was the the road leading east from Moscow, along which political prisoners were transported to Siberia.

p97, SRs were members of the Socialist Revolutionary Party.

p97, the Russian Communist Party (Bolsheviks) was the name of the CPSU from 1918 to 1925.

p97, Pulkovo Observatory near Leninigrad took part in observations of the planet Mars during the Great Apposition of 1924.

p105, Father Gapon was a Russian Orthodox priest who founded an organisation called 'the Assembly of Russian Factory Workers of St. Petersburg'; in 1905 he led a mass procession of workers to the tsar's palace where they were massacred by the tsar's troops. The day became known as 'Bloody Sunday'.

p105, Mukden is a city in China where Tsarist armies suffered a famous defeat during the Russo-Japanese War of 1905. Tsushima is an island in the Straits of Korea where the Japanese forces sank a large Russian naval detachment.

p105, Presnya is street in Moscow, the site of street fighting during the revolutionary uprising of 1905.

p107, in 1905 the Tsar Nicholas II issued a manifesto in which the people were promised 'freedom of speech.'

p107, FV Dubasov (1845-1912) was the Governor-general of Moscow who organized the suppression of the December uprising of 1905.

p109, GV Plekhanov (1856-1918) was a prominent figure in the Social-Democratic movement, a philosopher and literary critic. After the defeat of the Russian revolution of 1905, he declared that it had been wrong to begin the uprising, for which he was criticised by Lenin.

p113, Poltava and Plevna are cities in the Ukraine and Bulgaria where in 1709 and 1877 the Tsarist armies were victorious.

p113, Zimmerwald in Switzerland was the site of the world socialist conference held in September 1915. The manifesto adopted at the conference called on European workers to oppose the war and to fight for peace without annexations and contributions.

p119, Hohenzollern was the dynastic name of the German Kaiser Wilhelm II.

p121, Nevsky Prospekt is a central thoroughfare in St Petersburg.

p121, PI Milyukov (1859-1943) was the leader of the Cadet party, which advocated the continuance of the war until Russia had captured the Dardanelles. During the February revolution of 1917, he attempted to restore the monarchy by crowning prince Mikhail tsar.

p129, AF Kerensky (1881-1970) was the leader of the Provisional Government in Russia in 1917.

p123, BV Savinkov (1875-1925) was a member of the SR party, who took part in a counter-revolutionary plot in 1918.

p123, the Mensheviks were an oppositional trend inside the RSDLP.

p123, Liteyny Prospekt is a street in St Petersburg.

p127, MF Kshesinskaya (1872-1971) was ballerina. In 1917 the building presented to her by Tsar Nicholas II became the headquarters of the Central Committee of the RSDLP.

p129, on July 3, 1917 Petrograd workers, soldiers and sailors held a peaceful demonstration demanding the transfer of power to the Soviets. It was dispersed by gunfire at the orders of the Provisional Government.

p129, GE Zinoviev (1883-1936) was a member of the Central Committee of the RSDLP (B),

p135, the Smolny Institute was the headquarters of the October Revolution.

p137, the Aurora was the name of the battleship which fired the artillery shot that led to the storming of Winter Palace, which housed the Provisional Government.

p141, Dukhonin and Kornilov (1870- 1918) were Tsarist generals who attempted to crush the revolution.

p141, AI Guchkov (1862-1936) was a minister in the Provisional Government.

p141, the Decrees On Peace and On Land and the Decision on the Formation of a Workers' and Peasants' Government were the first documents to be issued by the revolutionary authorities.

p147, during the Civil War the counter-revolutionary forces were often depicted on posters as a many-headed hydra. One of Mayakovsky's 'Windows of ROSTA' also features a counter-revolutionary hydra.

p147, Denikin, Kolchak and Wrangel were Tsarist military leaders who at different periods of the Civil War headed the struggle against Soviet power.

p149, on August 30, 1918, after a meeting at Michelson's works in Moscow, Lenin was shot and severely wounded by SR member Fanny Kaplan.

p155, the NEP (New Economic Policy) was launched in 1921, aimed at promoting the recovery and development of the Russian economy.

p165, Mamontov was a Tsarist general, and one of the leaders of armed struggle against Soviet power in the Civil War, renowned for ruthless reprisals against peaceful citizens.

p165, MI Kalinin (1875-1919) led the session of the 11th All-Russian Congress of Soviets at which Lenin's death was announced.

p184, NK Krupskaya (1868-1939) was Lenin's wife.

p187, the Spasskaya clock-tower is in the Kremlin.

p189, NI Muralov (1886-1938) was the commander of the Moscow Military District in 1924.